More Crocheted SOCKS

16 All-New Designs

Janet Rehfeldt with Mary Jane Wood

Martingale®
& COMPANY

More Crocheted Socks: 16 All-New Designs
© 2010 by Janet Rehfeldt with Mary Jane Wood
Martingale & Company®

19021 120th Ave. NE, Suite 102
Bothell, WA 98011 USA
www.martingale-pub.com

Printed in China
15 14 13 12 11 10   8 7 6 5 4 3 2 1

Library of Congress Cataloging-in-Publication Data is available upon request.

ISBN: 978-1-60468-012-6

MISSION STATEMENT
Dedicated to providing quality products and service to inspire creativity.

CREDITS
President & CEO ✳ Tom Wierzbicki
Editor in Chief ✳ Mary V. Green
Managing Editor ✳ Tina Cook
Developmental Editor ✳ Karen Costello Soltys
Technical Editor ✳ Ursula Reikes
Copy Editor ✳ Marcy Heffernan
Design Director ✳ Stan Green
Production Manager ✳ Regina Girard
Illustrators ✳ Tim Maher & Laurel Strand
Cover & Text Designer ✳ Adrienne Smitke
Photographer ✳ Brent Kane

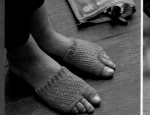

Contents

Acknowledgments

I'm always amazed at the number of people involved in putting a book together. From the concept to the final product, it takes a great many contributing all manner of talents. To everyone at Martingale & Company: for the hard work and dedication given to bringing *More Crocheted Socks* to the bookshelves: heartfelt thanks to all of you. What a great group of people to work with!

Although it's impossible to list everyone, there are a few people I would like to acknowledge, giving thanks and appreciation for their support and contributions.

Karen Costello Soltys, acquisitions and development editor: Thank you so much for the opportunity to write a follow-up to *Crocheted Socks!* I truly did enjoy this project.

Ursula Reikes, technical editor: Thank you for all your patience and the awesome way you transition words and instructions into something magical.

Lois Blanchard, model maker: Thank you for all your hard work not only crocheting models for me, but also for your helpful suggestions.

Tim Maher, illustrator: Thank you so much for the use of your illustrations once more and for reworking and tweaking several for a fresh look.

Introduction

Socks are still the *in* thing to make and wear. Look around waiting rooms, buses, trains, and planes, and you'll see hooks or needles flying and socks being made. And crocheting socks is even more popular than it was when *Crocheted Socks!* (Martingale & Company) was published in 2003.

While working on *Crocheted Socks!*, although yarn companies were already clamoring to meet the demand for a good variety of sock yarns, we were still having to use other types of yarn in order to come up with a large assortment of designs. Sock yarns now come in so many choices, including self-patterning colorways for stripes, Fair Isle, jacquard, or random effects, as well as a wide range of fiber contents, such as bamboo, soy, silk, alpaca, wool, cotton, acrylic, and even chitin (fiber derived from the outer skeleton of insects and shrimp and crab shells), and some yarn manufacturers are even pampering us by finishing their yarns with jojoba and/or aloe vera. Walking into a yarn shop or browsing sock yarns on the Web is like coming upon a theme park and trying to figure out what attraction to experience first. What could be more enticing than this wonderland of sock yarn that awaits us all?

For *More Crocheted Socks*, we kept the shaping used for knitted socks along with the beautiful stitch patterns of crochet in harmony to create comfortable, stylish, and great-fitting socks for crocheters. A couple of new features have been added for you, including an afterthought heel and a toeless, heelless sock for those into yoga and spa days.

It was so much fun picking out and working with the wide variety of yarns used for the socks in this book, and I hope that you have as much enjoyment in crocheting the socks as I had in bringing them to you.

—Janet Rehfeldt

Sock Basics

If you want your socks to wear and fit well, select sock yarns that contain some nylon (sometimes listed as polyamide); they'll wear better than yarns without nylon. If you fall in love with a yarn that doesn't have nylon, you can still use it for socks. If you do, you may want to run a thin elastic thread or Wooly Nylon serger thread along with the yarn when crocheting the cuff to help your socks stay up better.

Reinforcing heels and toes is optional. Crocheting a reinforcement yarn into the heel or toe will give a little extra strength when socks are worn in boots and/or if they get a lot of wear. A few yarn companies include matching reinforcement yarn with each skein.

Yarn amounts given in the materials section of the patterns are based on the circumference of the sock leg, the height of the sock leg, and the length of the sock foot. For women's shoe sizes over 8½ and men's shoe sizes over 11½, I recommend that you purchase additional yarn.

SPIFFY TOOLS

It doesn't take special gadgets to crochet socks, but some of these tools can be helpful.

* Crochet hooks can vary in size from one manufacturer to the next. For example, a G hook may be 4.00 mm from one manufacturer and 4.25 mm from a different manufacturer. The hook sizes listed in the materials section of each pattern are given in both U.S. and metric sizes, as in size E-4 (3.5 mm). Be sure to use a hook to match the metric size or the size needed to match the required gauge.

* Stitch markers are useful in marking where to work increases, decreases, and the beginning of rounds (see "Working with Markers" on page 61).

* Row counters are handy for tracking rows on stitch-pattern repeats and the number of times you may need to increase or decrease.

* A thread-cutter pendant is perfect for cutting yarn, especially when traveling.

* A good tape measure is a must for taking accurate measurements and checking your gauge.

* Large, blunt-end needles are necessary for weaving in ends and finishing toes, afterthought heels, and cuffs.

* Big "Eye" beading needles are used for stranding beads onto your project yarn. They're very thin needles with a split down the center of the shaft for threading your yarn.

Yarn-Weight Symbol and Category Name	0 Lace	1 Super Fine	2 Fine	3 Light
Types of Yarn in Category	Fingering 10-count crochet thread	Sock, Fingering, Baby	Sport, Baby	DK, Light Worsted
Crochet Gauge* Range in Single Crochet to 4"	32 to 42 double crochets**	21 to 32 sts	16 to 20 sts	12 to 17 sts
Recommended Hook in Metric Size Range	Steel 1.6 to 1.4 mm; Regular hook 2.25 mm	2.25 to 3.5 mm	3.5 to 4.5 mm	4.5 to 5.5 mm
Recommended Hook in U.S. Size Range	Steel 6, 7, 8; Regular hook B-1	B-1 to E-4	E-4 to 7	7 to I-9

* These are guidelines only. The above reflect the most commonly used gauges and needle or hook sizes for specific yarn categories.

** Lace-weight yarns are usually knit or crocheted on larger needles and hooks to create lacy openwork patterns. Accordingly, a gauge range is difficult to determine. Always follow the gauge stated in your pattern.

SOCK CONSTRUCTION

Sock construction is pretty basic and straightforward. The patterns are crocheted from either the cuff down to the toe, referred to as top-down socks, or from the toe up to the cuff, referred to as toe-up socks. The parts of a sock consist of the cuff, leg, heel, foot, and toe.

Sock Terminology
Sock with Heel Flap and Gusset

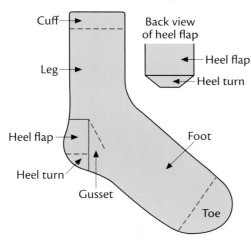

Sock with Short-Row or Afterthought Heel

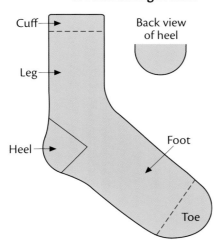

Cuffs

Cuffs are made in one of two ways. Because the sock must be able to fit over the foot, around the arch and heel, the cuff needs to be able to stretch a bit. Using a standard crochet chain will not give you the elasticity or stretch of a double-crochet foundation (see page 61)

Sock cuff worked in the round: Begin by using a double-crochet foundation rather than a standard chain. Then work front and back post stitches to create ribbing.

Sideways cuff worked in rows: Work with single crochet or slip stitches in the back loop of the stitches. Because slip stitches tend to lie on top of the previous row or round, tilt the work slightly toward you to make the stitches easier to see. Work slip stitches loosely and uniform in size to keep your cuff from being uneven. Once the cuff is complete, you'll crochet along the long edge of the cuff to begin the leg portion. Space your stitches evenly along the edge of the cuff for a smooth transition from the cuff to the leg.

Legs

Sock legs are crocheted in the round from the top down or bottom up. The exception is Over the Hills and Through the Woods (page 18), which is crocheted side to side using slip stitches.

Heels

Three heel-shaping styles are used in the socks: heel flap with gusset shaping, short-row heel, and afterthought heel. Before you begin the heel for a sock worked from the toe up, or for an afterthought heel, fold the sock flat with the toe centered and positioned correctly on your sock so that your heel, when finished, will be centered at the back of the foot. The exceptions are Over the Hills and Through The Woods on page 18 and the spa version of A Moment of Zen on page 42.

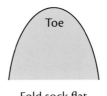

Fold sock flat
to position toe correctly.

Heel flap with gusset shaping: This consists of a rectangular flap that comes down around the back of the heel. The section at the bottom of the heel is called the heel turn. The heel turn is crocheted with decreases to shape the heel at the bottom so that it cups under the heel of your foot. A gusset section incorporates the heel flap into the sock foot by adding stitches along the side edges of the heel. Crocheting these stitches together where the heel meets the front of the foot creates a triangular wedge, decreasing the gusset section to fit the foot. This is one area where stitch markers are very helpful (see "Working with Markers" on page 61).

Short-row heel: This is made using a stair-step method that results in a heel similar to the heel of a commercial sock. Decreases are made by leaving unworked stitches at the end of each row. Stitches are then worked into these unworked stitches, one row at a time, to increase the heel back to the required number of stitches. You may want to place stitch markers in the unworked stitches to use as a guide for where to work the stitches.

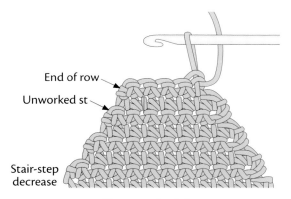

Short-row heel decreases

(Labels on image: End of row, Unworked st, Stair-step decrease)

NOTE:

You may find that when you work a short-row heel, you'll get a small hole or gap at one side where the heel meets the foot front. To eliminate this, work an additional slip stitch into the foot front on the next-to-last row of the heel. When working the first round of the foot (or the leg on toe-up socks), decrease the extra slip stitch by working it with the first stitch on the heel to keep your stitch count correct.

When working stitches along the side edges, insert the hook through a portion of the stitch while being careful not to split the yarn. Do not insert your hook around the post of a stitch or in the space between rows, as this will make an edge that looks sloppy and will leave holes.

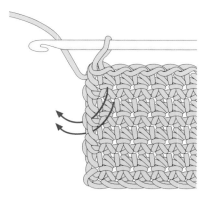

Afterthought heel: This is done by leaving one half of the stitches unworked, chaining the same number of stitches, then joining the chain to the front foot stitches, thereby creating an opening. For the heel (usually added after the remainder of the sock is completed), work stitches evenly around the heel opening, and then decrease at the side edges of the heel to the number of stitches indicated in your pattern.

Toes

To create a nearly invisible beginning for socks worked from the toe up, slip stitch into the bottom loop (or hump) of the beginning chain. Work slip stitches the same size as the beginning chain stitches. This is a foundation row that closes and neatens up the toe and is not counted as the first round of the toe.

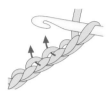

Begin the first round of the toe by pivoting your work and crocheting in the top loops of the actual chain. Work your first single-crochet stitch of round 1 in the first chain that was made.

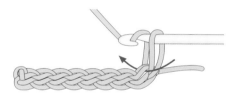

Continue to work single-crochet stitches along the chain, pivot the work, and single crochet in each slip stitch of the foundation row.

When working in the round, your work will naturally spiral unless you keep the decreases or increases at the side edges. If the toe stitches spiral into the foot, you'll have an uncomfortable and poorly fitting sock. Place markers at each end of the piece to mark the side edges of the toe; this will keep increases positioned correctly while shaping the toe. Move the markers with each round to keep them at the side edges of the foot. This may or may not be at the same decrease or increase of the round just completed. It may be one or two stitches to either side (see "Working with Markers" on page 61).

MAKING CUSTOM-FITTED SOCKS

If you can measure the foot, first follow the directions in "Taking Measurements" on page 11. Once you have the measurements, turn to "Finished Dimensions" in the sock pattern and refer to the circumference measurements for either the leg or the foot to determine which size sock to make.

For top-down socks, follow the pattern directions based on the measurement for the leg circumference; find the measurement that most closely matches your measurement and follow the corresponding directions for the entire sock. There is a degree of stretch in the leg, so you would normally work your leg 1" to 1½" narrower than your measurement, depending on the give of the stitch structure. You want the leg to fit comfortably, yet not fall.

For toe-up socks, follow the pattern directions based on the measurement for the foot circumference; find the measurement that most closely matches your measurement and follow the corresponding directions for the entire sock, working 1" to 1½" narrower than your measurement.

Try the sock on often while making it so that you can make sure the sock fits. In most of the patterns, you can make adjustments to the leg and foot circumference without disrupting the pattern stitch by decreasing or increasing one or two stitches.

If you cannot measure the foot, ask the recipient of the sock for his or her shoe width (narrow, medium, wide, extra wide) and shoe size. Refer to the shoe-width chart on page 10 to determine the approximate foot-circumference measurements. Allowing 1" to 1½" for the degree of stretch for both top-down and toe-up socks, match the chart measurement with one of the foot-circumference measurements in the pattern (see section labeled "Finished Dimensions" in pattern) and follow the corresponding directions for the entire sock. Listed after shoe width in the following chart is shoe size, which you can use to determine the approximate finished length of the sock foot from heel to toe. You'll need this information when you're crocheting the foot of the sock. The finished length of the sock foot is generally ½" to ¾" shorter than the actual length of the wearer's foot.

Pattern Sizing

The measurements listed in the following charts are based on standardized measurements for men's and women's shoe widths and shoe sizes.

SHOE WIDTH				
Approximate Foot Circumference at Ball of Foot (B on diagram, page 11)				
Women				
Shoe Width	Narrow	Medium	Wide	Extra Wide
Approx. Foot Circumference	6¾" to 7¼"	7½" to 8½"	9" to 9½"	9¾" to 11¼"
Men				
Shoe Width	Narrow	Medium	Wide	Extra Wide
Approx. Foot Circumference	8½" to 8¾"	9" to 10"	10½" to 11"	12" to 13"

SHOE SIZE		
Women's Shoe Size (Standard American)	Measurement of Actual Foot	Finished Length of Sock Foot
4 to 4½	8⅜"	7¾" to 8"
5 to 5½	8¾"	8¼" to 8½"
6 to 6½	9"	8½" to 8¾"
7 to 7½	9⅜"	9" to 9¼"
8 to 8½	9¾"	9¼" to 9½"
9 to 9½	10"	9½" to 9¾"
10 to 10½	10⅜"	10" to 10¼"
11 to 11½	10¾"	10¼" to 10½"
Men's Shoe Size (Standard American)	Measurement of Actual Foot	Finished Length of Sock Foot
8 to 9	10" to 10½"	9½" to 10"
10 to 11	10½" to 11"	10" to 10½"
12 to 13	11¼" to 11¾"	10½" to 11¼"
14	12"	11¼" to 11½"

Taking Measurements

Take measurements of your foot or the person's foot you plan to crochet socks for.

A While standing, measure up the leg from the floor to the height of the sock listed in the pattern. Measure the circumference of the actual leg to determine the circumference of the sock leg. There is a degree of stretch in the leg, so you would normally work your leg 1" to 1½" narrower than your measurement, depending on the give of the stitch structure.

B Measure the circumference of the foot at B, around the ball of the foot. The finished sock should be about 1" to 1½" narrower than the measurement for B.

C While standing, measure the foot from the back of the heel to the longest toe for the actual foot length (heel to toe). Your finished sock foot length should be ½" to ¾" shorter than the measurement for C.

D For toe-up socks, while standing, measure the foot from the longest toe to just below the ankle to determine where to begin the heel.

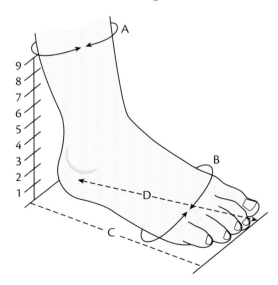

Calculating Your Gauge

Take the time to make a gauge swatch. When working in the round, your gauge will be slightly different than when working back and forth; it's recommended that you work your swatch in the round.

Make a chain of 24 stitches and slip stitch into the first chain to form a circle. Make sure you do not twist the chain. Work the leg pattern for 10 rows. Measure the circumference of the swatch. Divide the 24 stitches by the circumference measurement for the number of stitches per inch. Measure the length of the swatch. Divide the 10 rows by the length measurement for the number of rows per inch.

If you have more stitches per inch than the required gauge, try a larger hook. If you have fewer stitches per inch, try a smaller hook. If your stitches match but your rows are slightly off, it's usually a matter of correcting your tension. If you have fewer rows than listed in the pattern, tighten up your tension. If you have more rows, loosen up a bit.

If your foot pattern is different than your leg pattern, you may want to work a separate swatch for the foot.

CARE AND HANDLING

Crocheted socks are special and unique, so care should be taken when putting them on and laundering them. The following tips will help keep crocheted socks looking their best.

Trying on Socks

When trying on socks, inchworm them onto your foot like a nylon stocking—do not pull them on from the cuffs. Crocheted socks are not as elastic as knit socks, and the socks will stretch a little after working with them and checking them for fit; squeeze them gently to restore their shape.

Washing Tips

Wash your socks following the yarn-label instructions. If using a washing machine, turn your socks inside out and place them in a lingerie bag. If you find your wool or cotton socks feel harsh, use fabric softener or a capful of hair conditioner in the final rinse cycle to soften them up. Shape and lay the socks flat to dry.

Simple Simon

Designed by Janet Rehfeldt

The rich tapestry of colors and textures using front- and back-loop half double crochets make this sock a delightful experience to crochet. Simple Simon will walk you through all the basics of crocheting a sock from cuff to toe, with a heel flap and gusset. The stitch texture also looks great in solid colors.

Skill level: Easy ◼◼◻◻

FEATURED TECHNIQUES

* Top-down method
* Double-crochet-foundation-stitch cuff
* Heel flap with gusset

MATERIALS

1 skein of Sockin' Sox from Plymouth Yarn (60% superwash wool, 25% bamboo, 15% nylon; 100 g/3.5 oz; 436 yds/398 m) in color 003 (1)

Size D-3 (3.25 mm) crochet hook for cuff, heel flap, and toe

Size E-4 (3.5 mm) crochet hook for leg, gusset, and foot or size required for gauge

3 stitch markers

GAUGE

6.5 hdc and 4 rnds = 1" in patt with E hook

FINISHED DIMENSIONS

(with Sock Folded Flat)

Circumference of leg (unstretched): 6½ (7¼, 8½, 9¾)"

Circumference of foot (unstretched): 6½ (7¼, 8½, 9⅝)"

Floor to cuff: 8"

NOTE:

Do not sl st rnds closed and do not ch 1 at beg of rnds and rows unless instructed. A row counter is very helpful while working the gusset section.

CUFF

Rnd 1: With D hook, ch 3 (count as dc), dcf in 3rd ch from hook, work additional 40 (46, 54, 62) dcf, sl st in 3rd ch of beg ch 3 to form a circle and close rnd. [42 (48, 56, 64) dcf]

Rnds 2–6: FPdc around first 2 dc, BPdc around next 2 dc, *FPdc around next 2 dc, BPdc around next 2 dc; rep from * around, sl st in first dc to close rnd.

LEG

Rnd 1: Change to E hook, sk first dc, fl hdc in next dc, PM for beg of rnds, *bl hdc in next dc, fl hdc in next dc; rep from * around. [41 (47, 55, 63) hdc]

Rnd 2: Bl hdc in first hdc, *fl hdc in next hdc, bl hdc in next hdc; rep from * around.

Rnd 3: Fl hdc in first hdc, *bl hdc in next hdc, fl hdc in next hdc; rep from * around.

Rep rnds 2 and 3 until sock measures 5" from beg, end with rnd 3 of patt. Sl st in next st on last rnd.

HEEL FLAP

Row 1: Change to D hook, ch 1, sc in same st as sl st join in last rnd, sc in next 17 (21, 25, 27) sts. PM in next st on front foot section and note that it will be a fl hdc when you begin the gusset section. Turn. [18 (22, 26, 28) sc] Rem sts unworked.

Row 2 (WS): Ch 1, sc in each st across, turn.

Rep row 2 until heel measures 2½" to 2¾", ending with a WS row; do not fasten off.

HEEL TURN

Row 1 (RS): Ch 1, sc in first sc, *sc2tog twice, sc in next 8 (4, 6, 7) sc; rep from * 0 (1, 1, 1) time, sc2tog twice, sc in last sc, turn. [14 (16, 20, 22) sts]

Rows 2 and 3: Ch 1, sc in first sc, sc2tog, sc to last 3 sc, sc2tog, sc in last sc, turn. [10 (12, 16, 18) sts]

Row 4: Ch 1, sc in first 3 (4, 6, 7) sc, sc2tog twice, sc in last 3 (4, 6, 7) sc, turn. [8 (10, 14, 16) sc]

Row 5: Ch 1, sc in first sc, sc2tog 1 (1, 2, 2) times, sc to last 3 (3, 5, 5) sc, sc2tog 1 (1, 2, 2) times, sc in last sc; do not turn. [6 (8, 10, 12) sc]

GUSSET

Rnd 1: Work 18 sc evenly spaced along right edge of heel flap, PM, remove marker from first top foot st, change to E hook and work in patt across 23 (25, 29, 35) top foot sts beg with fl hdc. Change to D hook and work 18 sc evenly spaced along left-side edge of heel flap, PM in first sc on left side of heel flap, sc in 6 (8, 10, 12) sc heel sts, PM in last sc made to mark beg of rnds. Move markers with each rnd. Change to E hook. [65 (69, 75, 83) sc]

Rnd 2: Hdc to 3 sts prior to first marker, hdc2tog twice, work in established patt across top of foot beg with bl hdc, hdc2tog twice, hdc in rem heel sts. [61 (65, 71, 79) sts]

Rnd 3: Hdc to 3 sts prior to first marker, hdc2tog twice, work in established patt across top of foot beg with fl hdc, hdc2tog twice, hdc in rem heel sts. [57 (61, 67, 75) sts]

Rep rnds 2 and 3 until 41 (49, 55, 63) sts rem.

Next rnd: Hdc to 1 st prior to first marker, hdc2tog 0 (1, 0, 0) time, work in established patt across top of foot, hdc2tog 0 (1, 0, 0,) time, hdc in rem heel sts, then hdc to first gusset marker, hdc in marked st, PM for new beg of rnds. Remove other 2 markers. [41 (47, 55, 63) hdc]

FOOT

Cont with E hook and working in established patt, rep rnds 2 and 3 of leg patt until foot measures 2" from longest toe.

TOE

Remove beg-of-rnd marker. Fold sock so heel is positioned correctly on foot (see page 62). PM at each side edge of foot. Move side markers with each round to keep at side edges. Change to D hook, work in patt to center back of foot, 2 hdc in next st, PM for new beg of rnds. [42 (48, 56, 64) hdc]

Rnd 1: *Hdc in each st to 2 (2, 4, 4) sts prior to side-edge marker, hdc2tog 1 (1, 2, 2) times, hdc in marked st, hdc2tog 1 (1, 2, 2) times; rep from * once, hdc in rem sts to end of rnd. [38 (44, 48, 56) hdc]

Rnd 2: *Hdc in each st to 2 sts prior to side-edge marker, hdc2tog, hdc in marked st, hdc2tog; rep from * once, hdc in rem sts to end of rnd. [34 (40, 44, 52) hdc]

Rep rnd 2 until 18 (20, 24, 24) sts rem, work to closest side-edge marker and sl st in marked st. Fasten off, sew toe.

Hello Sunshine

Designed by Janet Rehfeldt

Bright yellows and a variety of textures bring a sunny forecast to any day. Post stitches along the heel add even more interest. Oh, and there's a bonus that's bound to bring a smile to your face and put a bounce in your step: the yarn is finished with aloe vera to soften and pamper your skin while crocheting and wearing these socks.

Skill level: Easy ●■□□

FEATURED TECHNIQUES

* Top-down method
* Sideways slip-stitch cuff
* Heel flap with gusset

MATERIALS

1 (1, 2, 2) skeins of Sock-Ease from Lion Brand Yarn (75% superwash wool, 25% nylon; 100 g/3.5 oz; 438 yds/400 m) in color 204 Lemon Drop (1)

Size D-3 (3.25 mm) crochet hook for cuff, heel flap, and toe

Size E-4 (3.5 mm) crochet hook for leg, gusset, and foot or size required for gauge

3 stitch markers

GAUGE

5.75 sts and 6 rnds = 1" in leg patt with E hook

6.5 sts and 6 rnds = 1" in foot patt with E hook

FINISHED DIMENSIONS
(with Sock Folded Flat)

Circumference of leg (unstretched): 6¾ (7¾, 8¾, 9¾)"

Circumference of foot (unstretched): 6½ (7½, 8½, 9½)"

Floor to cuff: 8"

NOTE:

Do not sl st rnds closed and do not ch 1 at beg of rnds and rows unless instructed.

CUFF

Row 1: With D hook, ch 11, sl st in 2nd ch from hook, bl sl st in each rem ch, turn. [10 sl sts]

Row 2: Bl sl st in each st across, turn.

Rep row 2 until piece measures 6¼ (7¼, 8¼, 9¼)".

LEG

Leg is worked on the WS and then turned to the RS for heel.

Pivot cuff to work along long side edge of cuff.

Rnd 1 (RS): Change to E hook, work 38 (44, 50, 56) sc evenly spaced along cuff. Bring short ends tog, matching ends to form a circle, join with sl st in first sc. Sew cuff closed (see page 62). Turn work so WS is facing. [38 (44, 50, 56) sc]

Rnd 2: *Sc in next st, tr in next st; rep from * around.

Rnd 3: Sc in each st around.

Rnd 4: *Tr in next st, sc in next st; rep from * around.

Rnd 5: Sc in each st around.

Rep rnds 2–5 until sock measures 5" from beg; end with rnd 3 or 5 of patt. Sl st in next st on last rnd. Turn work to RS.

Treble-crochet tip:

To make the treble crochet easier to work and more even, after working the first 2 lps off the hook, hold the base of the st between the thumb and forefinger of your non-hook hand while working rem lps.

HEEL FLAP

Row 1 (RS): Change to D hook, ch 1, sc in same st as sl st in last rnd, sc in next 18 (20, 22, 24) sts, turn. [19 (21, 23, 25) sc] Rem sts unworked.

Row 2: Ch 1, sc around each st across, turn.

Row 3: Ch 1, sc in first 2 sc, *FPdc around next st 2 rows below, sc in next sc; rep from * to last sc, sc in last sc, turn.

Row 4: Ch 1, sc in each st across, turn.

Rep rows 3 and 4 until heel measures 2½" to 2¾", ending with a WS row; do not fasten off.

HEEL TURN

Row 1 (RS): Ch 1, sc in first sc, sc2tog twice, sc in next 3 (4, 4, 5) sc, sc2tog twice, sc in next 2 (3, 5, 6) sc, sc2tog twice, sc in last sc, turn. [13 (15, 17, 19) sc]

Row 2: Ch 1, sc in first 5 (7, 7, 8) sc, sc2tog, sc in last 6 (6, 8, 9) sc, turn. [12 (14, 16, 18) sc]

Row 3: Ch 1, sc in first sc, sc2tog, sc to last 3 sc, sc2tog, sc in last sc, turn. [10 (12, 14, 16) sc]

Row 4: Ch 1, sc in first sc, sc2tog, *sc in next 1 (2, 3, 4) sc, sc2tog; rep from * once, sc in last sc, turn. [7 (9, 11, 13) sc]

Row 5: Ch 1, sc in each sc across; do not turn. [7 (9, 11, 13) sc]

GUSSET

Rnd 1: Work 18 sc evenly spaced along left edge of heel flap, PM, on 19 (23, 27, 31) top foot sts (sc, hdc) in first st, *sk next st, (sc, hdc) in next st; rep from * across top foot sts, work 19 sc evenly spaced along right-side edge of heel flap, PM in first sc on right side of heel flap, sc in 7 (9, 11, 13) sc heel sts, PM in last sc to mark beg of rnds. Move markers with each rnd. [10 (12, 14, 16) mini clusters, 44 (46, 48, 50) sc; 64 (70, 76, 82) sts total]

Rnds 2 and 3: Change to E hook, sc to 3 sts prior to first gusset marker, sc2tog twice, *(sc, hdc) in next sc, sk next hdc; rep from * across top foot sts, at next gusset marker sc2tog twice, sc in rem heel sts. [56 (62, 68, 74) sts]

Rnd 4: Sc to 1 st prior to first gusset marker, sc2tog, *(sc, hdc) in next sc, sk next hdc; rep from * across top foot sts, at next gusset marker sc2tog, sc in rem heel sts. [54 (60, 66, 72) sts]

Rep rnd 4 until 42 (48, 54, 62) sts rem. Remove beg-of-rnd marker.

Next rnd: Sc to front foot sts, remove first gusset marker, (sc, hdc) in next sc, sk next hdc across top foot sts, remove next gusset marker, *(sc, hdc) in next st, sk next sc; rep from * around heel sts, PM in first sc in top foot sts for new beg of rnds. [42 (48, 54, 62) sts]

FOOT

Next rnd: *(Sc, hdc) in next sc, sk next hdc; rep from * around. Rep last rnd until foot measures 2" from longest toe.

TOE

Fold sock so heel is positioned correctly on foot (see page 62). PM at each side edge, move markers with each rnd to keep at side edges of foot.

Rnd 1: Change to D hook, sc in each sc around, then sc to center back of foot, PM to mark beg of rnds. [42 (48, 54, 62) sc]

Rnds 2–4: Sc to 2 sts prior to first marker, *sc2tog, sc in marked st, sc2tog; rep from * once, sc in rem sc. [30 (36, 42, 50) sc at end of rnd 4]

Rnd 5: Sc in each sc around.

Rep rnds 4 and 5 until 18 (20, 22, 22) sts rem; work to closest side edge. Fasten off, sew toe.

Over the Hills and Through the Woods

Designed by Janet Rehfeldt

This sock may be the softest sock you'll ever own, with the sport-weight alpaca creating a soft and luxurious sock that pampers your foot. This hiker sock is sized in two leg lengths, allowing the two-toned cuff to be folded down or rolled over the top of your short-style boot. And the stretch of the cuff and foot pattern gives a good range for sizing.

Skill level: Intermediate ◖■■■▭

FEATURED TECHNIQUES

* Top-down method
* Sideways slip-stitch cuff and leg
* Afterthought heel

MATERIALS

Short Leg

Sport Weight Alpaca from Blue Sky Alpacas (100% baby alpaca; 50 g/1.75oz; 110 yds/100 m) in the following colors: (**2**)

MC 2 (2, 3, 3, 3) skeins in color 500 Natural White

CC 1 (1, 2, 2, 2) skeins in color 520 Avocado

Long Leg

Sport Weight Alpaca from Blue Sky Alpacas in the following colors:

MC 3 (3, 3, 4, 4) skeins in color 540 Cappuccino

CC 1 (1, 2, 2, 2) skeins in color 542 Currant

Both Versions

Size E-4 (3.5 mm) crochet hook for ankle, heel, foot, and toe or size required for gauge

Size F-5 (3.75 mm) crochet hook for cuff and leg or size required for gauge

3 stitch markers

GAUGE

6.5 sts and 10.5 rows = 1" in bl sl st with F hook

5.6 sts and 7 rnds = 1" in ankle/foot patt with E hook

FINISHED DIMENSIONS
(with Sock Folded Flat)

Due to stitch structure, sock leg has up to 2½" stretch.

Circumference of leg (unstretched): 6¼ (7¼, 8½, 9¼, 10½)"

Circumference of foot (unstretched): 6⅜ (7½, 8½, 9⅝, 10¾)"

Floor to cuff:

Short leg: 4½"

Longer leg: 9"

> **NOTE:**
>
> Do not cut yarn at ends of rnds and rows, do not sl st rnds closed, and do not ch 1 at beg of rnds and rows unless instructed. When changing the color in sl st, bringing current color to front of the work before working the sl st puts the yarn in the correct position for use in the next row.

CUFF AND LEG

Shorter leg style is listed first with longer leg style in parentheses.

Row 1: With F hook and MC, ch 22 (34), pick up CC and work 15 more chs; bl sl st in 2nd ch from hook, bl sl st in next 12 chs, bring CC to front of work and drop, insert hook into bl of next ch, using MC work sl st in last CC ch, bl sl st in 22 (34) chs, turn. [36 (48) sl sts]

Row 2: Ch 1, bl sl st in first sl st, bl sl st in next 20 (32) sl sts, bring MC to front of work and drop, insert hook into bl of next sl st, using CC work sl st in last MC sl st, bl sl st in 14 CC sl sts, turn.

Row 3: Ch 1, bl sl st in first sl st, bl sl st in next 12 sl sts, bring CC to front of work and drop, insert hook into bl of next sl st, using MC work sl st in last CC sl st, bl sl st in 22 (34) MC sl sts, turn.

Rep rows 2 and 3 until piece measures 6¼ (7¼, 8½, 9¼, 10½)" from beg, ending with MC. Cut CC, leaving 6" tail.

ANKLE

Pivot cuff to work along long side edge of cuff.

Rnd 1: Change to E hook, work 36 (42, 48, 54, 60) sc evenly spaced along cuff. Bring ends tog to form a circle, sl st in first sc of rnd to close. [36 (42, 48, 54, 60) sc] Matching colors tog, sew leg and cuff closed (see page 62).

Rnd 2: Sc in first sc, PM for beg of rnds, hdc in next 2 sc, *sc in next sc, hdc in next 2 sc; rep from * around. Do not sl st closed. [36 (42, 48, 54, 60) sts]

Rnd 3: Hdc in first sc, sc in next 2 hdc, *hdc in next sc, sc in next 2 hdc ; rep from * around.

HEEL OPENING

Right Sock

Rnd 1: Loosely ch 18 (21, 24, 27, 30), sk 18 (21, 24, 27, 30) sts, *sc in next hdc, hdc in next 2 sc; rep from * around. [18 (21, 24, 27, 30) sts; 18 (21, 24, 27, 30) chs]

Rnd 2: (Hdc in next ch, sc in next 2 chs) 6 (7, 8, 9, 10) times, *hdc in next sc, sc in next 2 hdc; rep from * around. Do not cut MC.

Left Sock

Rnd 1: (Sc in next hdc, hdc in next 2 sc) 6 (7, 8, 9, 10) times, loosely ch 18 (21, 24, 27, 30), sk 18 (21, 24, 27, 30) sts. [18 (21, 24, 27, 30) sts; 18 (21, 24, 27, 30) chs]

Rnd 2: Hdc in first sc, sc in next 2 hdc, (hdc in next sc, sc in next 2 hdc) 5 (6, 7, 8, 9) times, (hdc in next ch, sc in next 2 chs) 6 (7, 8, 9, 10) times. Do not cut MC.

AFTERTHOUGHT HEEL

When working into bottom of chs on heel opening, catch the first rnd of bottom of foot too, to better support the sts.

Fold sock flat with heel opening even across back of sock. PM at each side of heel opening, move markers with each rnd to keep at side edges of heel.

Rnd 1: Attach CC with sl st at corner edge of heel opening, making sure leg seam is on inside of leg. Evenly work 36 (42, 48, 54, 60) sc around heel opening.

Rnd 2: Sc in each st around.

Rnd 3: *Sc to 2 sts prior to marker, sc2tog, sc in marked st, sc2tog; rep from * once. [32 (38, 44, 50, 56) sc]

Rnds 4–6: Rep rnds 2 and 3 once, then rep rnd 2 once. [28 (34, 40, 46, 52) sc at end of rnd 6]

Rnds 7–10 (10, 11, 12, 13):
Rep rnd 3 until 16 (18, 20, 22, 24) sts rem. Work to closest side edge, fasten off, sew heel.

FOOT

Rnd 1: *Sc in next sc, hdc in next 2 sc; rep from * around.

Rnd 2: *Hdc in next sc, sc in next 2 hdc; rep from * around.

Rep rnds 1 and 2 of leg patt until foot measures 2½" from longest toe. Fasten off MC.

TOE

Fold sock so heel is positioned correctly on foot (see page 62). PM at each side edge. Move markers with each rnd to keep at sides of work.

Rnd 1: Attach CC with sl st at center back, sc in each st around.

Rnds 2–4: *Sc to 2 sts prior to marker, sc2tog, sc in next st, sc2tog; rep from * once, sc rem sts. [24 (30, 36, 42, 48) sc at end of rnd 4]

Rnd 5: Sc in each st around.

Rep rnds 4 and 5 until 16 (22, 24, 22, 24) sts rem, work to closest side edge. Fasten off, sew toe.

Witchy Woman

Designed by Janet Rehfeldt

When I saw this yarn, I just had to design a sock around the rich, vibrant colors. The lacy patterning, similar to a blackberry pattern, allows the tone-on-tone colorway to stand out and will call attention to your outfit no matter if you're in the mood for casual or dressy. You'll like this sock so much, you'll want to crochet more using other tonal colorways.

Skill level: Intermediate ⬤⬛⬛▢

FEATURED TECHNIQUES

* Toe-up method
* Afterthought heel
* Rolled cuff

MATERIALS

1 skein of Toe Jamz Sock Yarn from Happy Hands Hand Dyed Yarns (75% superwash merino, 25% nylon; 113 g/4 oz; 450 yds/411 m) in color Witchy Woman (**1**)

Size D-3 (3.25 mm) crochet hook or size required for gauge

3 stitch markers

GAUGE

6.75 esc and 4 rnds in patt = 1"

FINISHED DIMENSIONS

(with Sock Folded Flat)

Circumference of leg (unstretched): 6⅜ (7¼, 8¼, 9⅜)"

Circumference of foot (unstretched): 6⅜ (7¼, 8¼, 9⅜)"

Floor to cuff: 7" without cuff rolled down

NOTE:

Do not sl st rnds closed and do not ch 1 at beg of rnds or rows unless instructed.

TOE

Foundation row: Ch 10, working in bottom lp, sl st in second ch from hook, sl st in each ch. [9 (9, 11, 11) sl sts]

Rnd 1: Working in top lps of beg ch, sc in each ch, pivot work, sc in each sl st of foundation row. PM at each end to mark side edges of toe. Move markers with each rnd to keep at side edges of toe. [18 (18, 22, 22) sc]

Rnd 2: *Sc to 1 st prior to side marker, 2 sc in next sc, 1 sc in marked st, 2 sc in next st; rep from * once.[22 (22, 26, 26) sc]

Rnd 3: Sc in each st around.

Rep rnds 2 and 3 until 42 (46, 54, 62) sts rem, on last rnd sl st in first sc of rnd. Remove side-edge markers.

FOOT

Do not work ch tightly in rnds 1 and 3, do not work into the ch-1 sp, work into the top lps of the chs on rnd 2 of patt.

Rnd 1: (Esc, ch 1, esc) in next sc, PM at side edge for beg of rnds, *sk 2 sc, (esc, ch 1, esc) in next sc; rep from * to last 2 (0, 2, 1) sc, sk 2 (0, 2, 1) sc. [14 (16, 18, 21) shells]

Rnd 2: Sk next esc, *3 esc in next ch, sk next 2 esc; rep from* around to last esc, sk last esc. [42 (48, 54, 63) esc]

Rnd 3: Sk first esc, *(esc, ch 1, esc) in next esc, sk 2 esc; rep from * around to last esc, sk last esc. [14 (16, 18, 21) shells]

Rep rnds 2 and 3 until foot reaches just below anklebone or approx 2½" shorter than desired foot length, ending with rnd 3.

HEEL OPENING

Rnd 1: Fold sock so toe is positioned correctly on foot (see page 7). Sk next esc, *3 esc in next ch, sk next 2 esc; rep from * over next 6 (7, 8, 10) mini shells, loosely ch 21 (24, 27, 30), sk next 7 (8, 9, 10) mini shells [21 (24, 27, 33) esc; 21 (24, 27, 30) chs]

Rnd 2: Sk first esc, *(esc, ch 1, esc) in next esc, sk 2 esc; rep from * to heel opening, sk next esc and first ch on heel opening, (esc, ch 1, esc) in next ch, **sk next 2 chs, (esc, ch 1, esc) in next ch; rep from ** to last ch, sk last ch. [14 (16, 18, 21) mini shells]

LEG

Rep rnds 2 and 3 of foot patt until leg section measures 4½" from heel opening, ending with rnd 2.

CUFF

Work sl sts slightly loose, but not sloppy.

Rnd 1: *Sl st in next esc, esc in next esc; rep from * around to last 1 (1, 1, 0) st, (esc, sl st) in last 1 (1, 1, 0) st. [43 (49, 55, 63) sts]

Rnd 2: *Esc in next sl st, sl st in next esc; rep from * around.

Rnds 3–7: Rep rnd 2, ending with a sl st on last rnd. Fasten off. Allow cuff to naturally roll.

HEEL

Rnd 1: Fold sock, positioning toe correctly on foot (see page 7). PM at side edges of heel opening. Attach yarn at right edge of heel, evenly work 42 (48, 54, 64) sc around heel opening. Move markers with each rnd to keep at side edges of heel.

Rnd 2: *Sc in each sc to 2 sts prior to marker, sc2tog, sc in marked st, sc2tog; rep from * once. [38 (44, 50, 60) sc]

Rnd 3: Sc in each st around.

Rep rnds 2 and 3 until 22 (24, 26, 28) sts rem, work to side edge of heel, sl st in marked st. Fasten off, sew heel.

A Little Zig, a Little Zag

Designed by Janet Rehfeldt

This is the perfect "boyfriend" sock to match that borrowed pair of jeans, sweater, or shirt that were so comfy they just naturally ended up in your closet. The migrating rib and modified basket weave creates a unisex look, and they're sized so you can share with the favorite someone you "just borrowed" those comfy clothes from. This design also looks great in solid colors.

Skill level: Intermediate ⬤■■▢

FEATURED TECHNIQUES

* ✳ Top-down method
* ✳ Sideways single-crochet cuff
* ✳ Short-row heel

MATERIALS

1 (1, 2, 2, 2, 2) Aussi Sock (90% Aussi merino, 10% nylon; 100 g/3.75 oz; 400 yds/367 m) in color WS23 Atlantic Weaves **1**

Size D-3 (3.25 mm) crochet hook for cuff, heel, foot, and toe or size required for gauge

Size E-4 (3.5 mm) crochet hook for leg

3 stitch markers

GAUGE

6.5 sts and 6 rnds = 1" in esc with D hook

FINISHED DIMENSIONS
(with Sock Folded Flat)

Due to ribbed leg structure, leg has approx 2" stretch.

Circumference of leg (unstretched): 6 (7¼, 8½, 9½, 10⅝, 11¾)"

Circumference of foot (unstretched): 6¼ (7½, 8¾, 9⅞, 11, 12)"

Floor to cuff: 8"

NOTE:

Do not sl st rnds closed and do not ch 1 at beg of rnds and rows unless instructed.

CUFF

Row 1: With D hook, ch 11, bl sc in 2nd ch from hook, bl sc in each ch, turn. [10 sc]

Row 2: Ch 1, bl sc in each sc, turn.

Rep row 2 until piece measures 5¾ (7, 8¼, 9¼, 10¼, 11¼)".

Next rnd: Pivot cuff, evenly work 40 (48, 56, 64, 72, 80) sc along side edge, bring ends tog, matching ends to form a circle, sl st in first sc to close rnd. Sew cuff.

LEG

Rnd 1: Change to E hook, dc in each st around. [40 (48, 56, 64, 72, 80) dc]

Rnd 2: FPdc around next st, BPdc around next 3 sts, *FPdc around next 5 sts, BPdc around next 3 sts; rep from * to last 4 sts, FPdc around last 4 sts. [40 (48, 56, 64, 72, 80) dc]

Rnd 3: FPdc around next 2 sts, BPdc around next 3 sts, *FPdc around next 5 sts, BPdc around next 3 sts; rep from * to last 3 sts, FPdc around last 3 sts.

Rnd 4: FPdc around next 3 sts, BPdc around next 3 sts, *FPdc around next 5 sts, BPdc around next 3 sts; rep from * to last 2 sts, FPdc around last 2 sts.

Rnd 5: FPdc around next 4 sts, BPdc around next 3 sts, *FPdc around next 5 sts, BPdc around next 3 sts; rep from * to last st, FPdc around last st.

Rnd 6: *FPdc around next 5 sts, BPdc around next 3 sts; rep from * around.

Rnd 7: BPdc around next st, FPdc around next 5 sts, *BPdc around next 3 sts, FPdc around next 5 sts; rep from * to last 2 sts, BPdc around last 2 sts.

Rnd 8: BPdc around next 2 sts, FPdc around next 5 sts, *BPdc around next 3 sts, FPdc around next 5 sts; rep from * to last st, BPdc around last st.

Rnd 9: *BPdc around next 3 sts, FPdc around next 5 sts; rep from * around.

Rnds 10–16: Work backward from rnd 8 to rnd 2.

Rnds 17–21: Rep rnds 2–6.

HEEL

Row 1: Change to D hook, PM in last st to mark top of foot, sl st in next st, sc in same st as sl st, sc in next 19 (23, 25, 29, 31, 35) sts, PM in next st to mark top of foot, turn. [20 (24, 26, 30, 32, 36) sc] Rem sts unworked.

Row 2 (WS): Ch 1, sc in first sc, sc in each sc across, leaving last st unworked, turn. [19 (23, 25, 29, 31, 35) sc]

Rep row 2 until 6 (8, 10, 12, 14, 16) sc rem.

HEEL INCREASE

Row 1 (WS): Sc in 6 (8, 10, 12, 14, 16) sc, sc in side edge of heel, sc in closest sk st on heel, sl st in side of heel, turn. [8 (10, 12, 14, 16, 18) sc]

Row 2: Sk sl st, sc in 8 (10, 12, 14, 16, 18) sc, sc in closest sk st on heel, sc in next closest sk st, sl st in side edge of heel, turn. [10 (12, 14, 16, 18, 20) sc]

Row 3: Sk sl st, sc in 10 (12, 14, 16, 18, 20) sc, sc in closest sk st on heel, sl st in side edge of heel, turn. [11 (13, 15, 17, 19, 21) sc]

Rep row 3 increasing to 18 (22, 24, 28, 30, 34) sc.

Next row: Sk sl st, sc in 18 (22, 24, 28, 30, 34) sc, sc in closest sk st on heel, sl st in side edge at base of heel next to marked st at top of foot, turn. [19 (23, 25, 29, 31, 35) sc]

Next row: Sk sl st, sc in 19 (23, 25, 29, 31, 35) sc, sc in closest sk st on heel, sl st in side edge at base of heel next to marked st at top of foot; do not turn. Remove markers. [20 (24, 26, 30, 32, 36) sc]

FOOT

Rnd 1 (RS): *Esc in next 2 sts on front foot, bl esc in next 2 sts, rep across 16 (20, 26, 30, 36, 40) more top foot sts, insert hook in sl st, YO, pull up lp, insert hook into sc on heel, YO, pull up lp, YO, pull through 2 lps (twice), esc in rem 19 (23, 25, 29, 31, 35) sc of heel. PM in first st for beg of rnds. [40 (48, 56, 64, 72, 80) esc]

Rnd 2: *Esc in next 2 esc, bl esc in next 2 esc; rep from * around.

Rnds 3 and 4: *Bl esc in next 2 esc, fl esc in next 2 esc; rep from * around.

Rnds 5 and 6: *Esc in next 2 esc, bl esc in next 2 esc; rep from * around.

Rep rnds 3–6 until foot measures 2" to 2½" from longest toe, ending with rnd 4 or 6. Do not fasten off.

TOE

Fold sock so that heel is positioned correctly (see page 62), PM at each side edge. Move markers with each rnd to keep at side edges. Work to center back of foot, PM for beg of rnds, sl st in next st.

Rnds 1–2 (2, 3, 4, 5, 6): *Sc to 2 sts prior to side-edge marker, sc2tog, sc in marked st, sc2tog; rep from * once, sc in rem foot sts. [32 (40, 44, 48, 52, 56) sc at end of rnd 2 (2, 3, 4, 5, 6)]

Next rnd: Sc in each st around.

Next rnd: *Sc to 2 sts prior to side-edge marker, sc2tog, sc in marked st, sc2tog; rep from * once, sc in rem foot sts [28 (36, 40, 44, 48, 52) sts].

Rep last 2 rnds until 20 (24, 24, 28, 28, 32) sts rem, then sc in each st around. Work to closest side edge. Fasten off, sew toe.

Victorian Daydream

Designed by Mary Jane Wood

Designed to be open and lacy, this sock lets a bit of your leg peek through. The simple yet elegant foot pattern, the delicate lace pattern of the leg, and the lovely shell cuff will bring to mind a bygone era. You'll want to show these socks off to all your friends. A light-colored yarn is best suited for this pattern to accentuate the lace pattern.

Skill level: Intermediate ■■■◻

FEATURED TECHNIQUES

* Toe-up method
* Short-row heel

MATERIALS

1 skein of Happy Feet Dye For Me from Plymouth Yarns (90% super-wash merino wool, 10% nylon; 125 g/4.5 oz; 480 yds/439 m) in color 99 Natural (**1**)

Size E-4 (3.5 mm) crochet hook or size required for gauge

3 stitch markers

GAUGE

5.25 sts and 3 rnds = 1" in foot patt

2 shells and 3 rnds = 1" in leg patt

FINISHED DIMENSIONS

(with Sock Folded Flat)

Circumference of leg (unstretched): 6¾ (8, 9, 10¼)"

Circumference of foot (unstretched): 6¾ (8, 9, 10¼)"

Floor to cuff: 7¾"

NOTE:

Do not sl st or ch at the end of the rnd unless otherwise instructed.

TOE

Foundation row: Ch 11 (14, 17, 20). Working in bottom lp, sl st in second ch from hook, sl st in each ch. [10 (13, 16, 19) sl sts]

Rnd 1: Working in top lps of beg ch, sc in each ch. Pivot work, sc in each sl st of foundation row. [20 (26, 32, 38) sc]

Rnd 2: PM at each end to mark side edges of toe. Move markers with each rnd to keep at side edges of toe. Sc to 1 st prior to side marker, *2 sc in next st, sc in marked st, 2 sc in next st; rep from * once. [24 (30, 36, 42) sc]

Rnd 3: Sc in each st.

Rnds 4–9: Rep rnds 2 and 3. [36 (42, 48, 54) sc at end of rnd 9] Remove markers.

Rnd 10: Sc in each st.

FOOT

Rnd 1: *Sc in next st, ch 1, sk next st; rep from * around.

Rnd 2: *Sc in next sc, esc in skipped st from rnd 1; rep from * around.

Rep rnds 1 and 2 until foot reaches just below anklebone or approx 2" less than desired foot length, ending with rnd 2.

HEEL

Fold sock so toe is positioned correctly on foot (see page 7). Sl st to side edge.

Row 1 (RS): Sc in next 18 (21, 24, 27) sts, turn. Rem sts unworked.

Row 2: Sc in each st, turn.

Row 3: Sc in each sc, leaving last st unworked, turn. [17 (20, 23, 26) sc]

Rep row 3 until 6 (9, 12, 15) sts rem.

HEEL INCREASE

Row 1: Sc in next 6 (9, 12, 15) sc, sc in side edge of heel, sc in closest unworked st down heel side, sl st in side edge below sc just made, turn. [8 (11, 14, 17) sc]

Row 2: Sk sl st, sc in next 8 (11, 14, 17) sc, sc in side edge of heel, sc in closest unworked st down heel side, sl st in side edge below sc just made, turn. [10 (13, 16, 19) sc]

Row 3: Sk sl st, sc in each sc, sc in next closest unworked st down heel side, sl st in side edge below sc just made, turn. [11 (14, 17, 20) sc]

Rep row 3 until 18 (21, 24, 27) sc rem.

Next 2 rows: Sk sl st, sc in each sc, sc in next closest unworked st at side, sl st in next st on foot front, turn. [20 (23, 26, 29) sc in last row]

LEG

Rnd 1 (RS): *Work 3 hdc in next st, sk 2 sts; rep from * around, sl st in first 2 sts of rnd. PM in first hdc to mark beg of rnds. [36 (42, 48, 54) hdc]

Rnd 2: Sk first 2 sts of rnd, *3 hdc in next st, sk 2 sts; rep from * around.

Rep rnd 2 until sock leg measures 4½".

CUFF

At end of rnds, always sl st in first st of rnd and beg next rnd in same st as sl st.

Rnd 1: Hdc in each st.

Rnds 2 and 3: *Dc in next st, sk next st, ch 1; rep from * around.

Rnd 4: *Work 6 tr in next dc, sk next 5 sts; rep from * around. Fasten off.

Hoops, Nets, and Frills

Designed by Janet Rehfeldt

Regardless of whether you're playing hoops, spiking a ball, or swinging a putter or a racket, you'll snazz up the court or greens with this sporty little number designed with a little frothy frill to liven up your game. The elastic yarn makes this anklet comfortable to wear, and you can crochet your socks with or without the frills.

Skill level: Experienced ◼◼◼▶

FEATURED TECHNIQUES

* Top-down method
* Double-crochet-foundation-stitch cuff
* Heel flap with gusset

MATERIALS

No Frills

1 (2, 2, 2) skeins of Stretch Socks from Patons Yarns (41% cotton, 39% wool, 13% nylon, 7% elastic; 50 g/1.75 oz; 230 yds/218 m) in color 31040 Licorice (**1**)

Frills

1 (2, 2, 2) skeins of Stretch Socks from Patons Yarns in color 31206 Kelp (**1**)

Both Versions

Size D-3 (3.25 mm) crochet hook or size required for gauge
3 stitch markers

GAUGE

4.25 (sc, ch-1 groups) and 6 rnds = 1"

FINISHED DIMENSIONS

(with Sock Folded Flat)

The elastic stretch yarn allows for 2" to 2½" stretch.

Circumference of ankle (unstretched): 6 (7, 8, 9)"

Circumference of foot (unstretched): 6½ (7½, 8½, 9¾)"

Floor to cuff: 4¾" excluding trim

NOTE:

Do not sl st rnds closed and do not ch 1 at beg of rnds and rows unless instructed. When working sl sts, count your sts often and do not work the sts tightly.

CUFF

Rnd 1: Ch 3 (count as dc), dcf in 3rd ch from hook, work additional 42 (46, 50, 56) dcf, sl st in 3rd ch of beg ch 3 to form a circle and close rnd. [44 (48, 52, 58) dcf]

Rnd 2–10: FPdc around first 2 dc, BPdc around next 2 dc, *FPdc around next 2 dc, BPdc around next 2 dc; rep from * around, sl st in first dc to close rnd. [44 (48, 52, 58) dc]

HEEL FLAP

Row 1 (RS): Ch 1, sc in same st as sl st join of rnd 10, sc in next 19 (23, 25, 25) sts, turn. [20 (24, 26, 26) sc] Rem sts unworked.

Row 2: Ch 1, sl st in first st, bl sl st in each st across, turn. [20 (24, 26, 26) sl sts]

Row 3: Ch 1, sl st in first st, fl sl st in each st across, turn.

Rep rows 2 and 3 until heel measures 2½" to 2¾", ending with a WS row; do not fasten off.

HEEL TURN

Work sc dec in both lps of st.

Row 1 (RS): Ch 1, sl st in first 1 (1, 2, 2) sts, sc2tog twice, *fl sl st in next 3 (2, 2, 2) sts, sc2tog twice; rep from * 1 (2, 2, 2)

times, sl st in last 1 (1, 2, 2) st, turn. [14 (16, 18, 18) sts]

Row 2: Ch 1, sl st in first st, sc2tog, *bl sl st in next 3 (4, 5, 5) sts, sc2tog; rep from * once, sl st in last st, turn. [11 (13, 15, 15) sts]

Row 3: Ch 1, sl st in first st, sc2tog, fl sl st in next 1 (2, 3, 3) sts, sc2tog, fl sl st in each of next 2 (3, 4, 4) sts, sc2tog, sl st in last st. Do not turn. [8 (10, 12, 12) sts]

GUSSET

Do not work into ch-1 sps, and do not count ch-1 sps unless otherwise instructed. Work sc dec in both lps of st.

Rnd 1: Work 16 sts evenly spaced along right edge of heel flap, PM, sc 1 (2, 2, 2) in first st on front foot, sc 22 (22, 24, 30) more top foot sts, sc 1 (2, 2, 2) in next st on front foot, work 16 sc evenly spaced along left-side edge of heel flap, PM in first sc on left side of heel flap, sc in 8 (10, 12, 12) heel sts, PM in last sc made to mark beg of rnds. Move markers with each rnd. [64 (68, 72, 78) sts]

Rnd 2: Fl sl st to 1 st prior to first marker, sc2tog, (sc, ch 1) in next 24 (26, 28, 34) sc across top of foot, sc2tog, fl sl st in rem heel sts. [62 (66, 70, 76) sts excluding ch-1 sps]

Rnd 3: Bl sl st to 1 st prior to first marker, sc2tog, (sc, ch 1, sk next ch-1 sp) in 24 (26, 28, 34) sc across top of foot, sc2tog, bl sl st in rem heel sts. [60 (64, 68, 74) sts]

Rnd 4: Fl sl st to 1 st prior to first marker, sc2tog, (sc, ch 1, sk next ch-1 sp) across top of foot, sc2tog, fl sl st in rem heel sts. [58 (62, 66, 72) sts]

Rep rnds 3 and 4, ending with rnd 4 (4, 4, 3) until 32 (38, 42, 48) sts rem, excluding ch-1 sps. Remove markers. [26 (28, 30, 36) sc; 6 (10, 12, 12) sl sts]

FOOT

Rnd 1: Bl sl st in each sl st along heel to front foot sts, (sc, ch 1) in next sc, PM for beg of rnds, (sc, ch 1, sk next ch-1 sp) in each sc across top of foot, sk next ch-1 sp, sk next st *(sc, ch 1) in next st, sk next st; rep from * around,

(sc, ch 1) in last st 0 (0, 1, 1) time. [28 (32,36, 42) sc]

Rnd 2: *(Sc, ch 1) in next sc, sk next ch-1 sp; rep from * around.

Rep rnd 2 until foot measures 2" from longest toe. Remove beg-of-rnd marker.

TOE

Work sc dec in both lps of st.

Fold sock so that heel is positioned correctly on foot (see page 62). PM at each side edge of foot. Move markers with each rnd to keep at side edges. Work in patt to center back of foot, sc in next sc, sl st in next ch-1 sp, PM for beg of rnds. Turn work so that WS of sock is facing you.

Rnd 1: Working in sc and ch-1 sps, *bl sl st in each st to 2 sts prior to side marker, sc2tog, bl sl st in next st, sc2tog; rep from * once, bl sl st in rem sts to end of rnd. [52 (60, 68, 80) sts]

Rnd 2: Bl sl st in each st around.

Rnd 3: *Bl sl st to 2 sts prior to side marker, sc2tog, bl sl st in next st, sc2tog; rep from * once, bl sl st in rem foot sts. [48 (56, 64, 76, sts]

Rep rnds 2 and 3 until 24 (24, 28, 28) sts rem. Fasten off. Turn work to RS facing you. Sew toe.

CUFF TRIM FOR FRILLS

Rnd 1: Attach yarn with sl st to cuffs at inner side of leg, *ch 5, sk 3 sts, sl st in next dc; rep from * around, sl st to first sl st.

Rnd 2: Sc 6 in each ch-5 sp around, sl st to first sc.

Rnd 3: Ch 3, sk first 2 sc, *(sc, ch 3, sc) in next sc, ch 3, sk 2 sc, sc in next sc, ch 3, sk next 2 sc; rep from * around. Fasten off.

Beaded Lace

Designed by Mary Jane Wood

Beaded lace and a picot edging make these a must-have addition to your sock collection. The elegant look is created by using a mix of crystal, matte, metallic-lined, and pearlized beads in shades of cream, clear, and topaz against a rich peach background. For a more casual look, try using beads in a contrasting color.

Skill level: Intermediate ◖■■▭

FEATURED TECHNIQUES

* Top-down method
* Double-crochet-foundation-stitch cuff
* Short-row heel

MATERIALS

1 skein of Aussi Sock (90% Aussi merino, 10% nylon, 100 g/3.75 oz; 400 yds/367 m) in color WS01 Peach Cobbler (**1**)

2 packets of Czech glass beads size 6/0 (10 g per packet) in cream topaz color and finish (shiny, matte, metallic, etc.) mix

Big "Eye" Needle (see page 6) to string beads (optional)

Size D-3 (3.25 mm) crochet hook or size required for gauge

3 stitch markers

GAUGE

6 sts and 5 rnds = 1" in leg patt

FINISHED DIMENSIONS
(with Sock Folded Flat)

Circumference of leg (unstretched): 7 (8, 9, 10)"

Circumference of foot (unstretched): 7 (8, 9, 10)"

Floor to cuff: 7"

NOTE:

Do not sl st rnds closed and do not ch 1 at beg of rnds and rows unless instructed.

SPECIAL STITCHES

Beaded half double crochet (bhdc): Bring bead down close to hook, YO, insert hook in indicated st, YO, pull though st, YO, pull through 3 lps on hook.

Beaded single crochet (bsc): Insert hook in indicated st, YO, pull through st, bring bead down close to hook, YO, pull through 2 lps on hook.

LEG

At end of rnds 1–4, sl st tightly in first st of rnd before turning work.

String 1 packet of beads onto yarn using a Big "Eye" needle, a beading needle, or dental floss threader.

Foundation rnd: Ch 3 (counts as first dc), work 41 (47, 53, 59) dcf, sl st in top of beg ch 3 to close rnd. [42 (48, 54, 60) dcf]

Rnd 1 (RS): Sl st in first 2 sts, (ch 4, dc) in same st as last sl st (counts as dc, ch 1, dc), sk 2 sts, *(dc, ch 1, dc) in next st, sk 2 sts; rep from * around, sl st in 3rd ch of beg ch 4, turn. [42 (48, 54, 60) sts]

Rnd 2: *Hdc in next dc, bhdc in next ch-1 sp, hdc in next dc; rep from *, sl st in first hdc, turn.

Rnd 3: Rep rnd 1.

Rnd 4: Hdc in each st and ch-1 sp, sl st in first hdc, turn.

Rep rnds 1–4 until leg measures 4½", ending with rnd 4.

HEEL

Row 1 (RS): Sc in next 21 (24, 27, 30) sts, turn. Rem sts unworked.

Row 2: Sc in each sc, turn.

Row 3: Sc in each sc, leaving last st unworked, turn. [20 (23, 26, 29) sc]

Rep row 3 until 9 (12, 15, 18) sts rem.

HEEL INCREASE

Row 1: Sc in next 9 (12, 15, 18) sc, sc in side edge of heel, sc in closest unworked st on heel, sl st in side edge of heel below sc just made, turn. [11 (14, 17, 20) sc]

Row 2: Sk sl st, sc in next 11 (14, 17, 20) sc, sc in side edge of heel, sc in closest unworked st on heel, sl st in side edge of heel below sc just made, turn. [13 (16, 19, 22) sc]

Row 3: Sk sl st, sc in each sc, sc in next closest unworked st on heel, sl st in side edge of heel, turn. [14 (17, 20, 23) sc]

Rep row 3 until 21 (24, 27, 30) sc rem.

Next 2 rows: Sk sl st, sc in each sc, sc in next closest unworked st on heel, sl st in next st on foot front, turn. [23 (26, 29, 32) sc at last row]

FOOT

Rnd 1 (RS): Sc in each sc around heel, sk sl st, sc in 19 (22, 25, 28) sts along front foot. [42 (48, 54, 60) sc] Fasten off.

With RS facing out, reattach yarn in middle of heel so joining will be on bottom of foot.

Rnd 2 (RS): Hdc in each sc around, sl st tightly in first st, turn.

Rnd 3: Sc in each st around, sl st tightly in first st, turn.

Rep rnds 2 and 3 until sock measures 2" from longest toe, ending with rnd 3.

TOE

Fold sock so heel is positioned correctly on foot (see page 62). PM on each side of sock. Move markers with each rnd to keep at side edges.

Rnd 1: *Hdc to 2 sts prior to marker, hdc2tog, hdc in marked st, hdc2tog; rep from * once, hdc in rem sts. [38 (44, 50, 56) hdc]

Rnd 2: *Sc to 2 sts prior to marker, sc2tog, sc in marked st, sc2tog; rep from * once, sc in rem sts. [34 (40, 46, 52) sc]

Rep rnds 1 and 2 until 18 (24, 30, 36) sts rem.

Next rnd: Sc in each st around. Fasten off. Sew toe.

CUFF

Rnd 1 (RS): Reattach yarn with sl st in any st on top of leg section. Sc in each st around, sl st in first st, turn. [42 (48, 54, 60) sc]

Rnd 2: *Bsc in next st, sc in next 5 sts; rep from * around, sl st in first st, turn.

Rnd 3: *(Sc, ch 2, sc) in next st, sk next 3 sts, (sc, ch 2, sc) in next st, (sc, ch 4, sc) in next st; rep from * around. Fasten off.

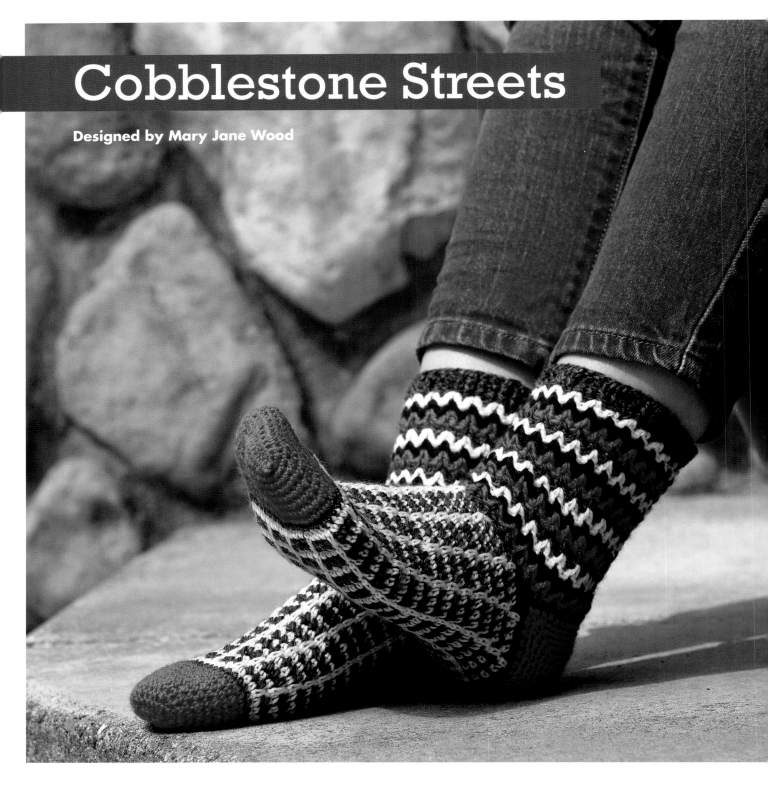

Cobblestone Streets

Designed by Mary Jane Wood

The pattern of this sock brings to mind cobblestone streets and flowered trellises. Though the foot may look complicated, only one color is used on each round, making an attractive multicolored effect. All colors are carried up with each round to alleviate loose ends. This sock is a great "stash buster" and a good way to use up your leftovers. Be sure to use contrasting colors for the best results.

Skill level: Intermediate ⬤■■▭

FEATURED TECHNIQUES

* Top-down method
* Double-crochet-foundation-stitch cuff
* Afterthought heel

MATERIALS

Wildfoote from Brown Sheep Company (75% wool 25% nylon; 50 g/1.75oz; 215 yds/197 m) in the following colors: [1]

A 1 skein of SY10 Vanilla

B 1 skein of SY05 Black Orchid

C 1 skein of SY26 Blue Blood Red

D 1 skein of SY29 Tom Cat

Size D-3 (3.25 mm) crochet hook for cuff, leg, heel, and foot or size required for gauge

Size E-4 (3.5 mm) crochet hook for making chain-over-heel opening

3 stitch markers

GAUGE

5.33 sts and 5.25 rnds = 1" in leg patt with D hook

5.33 sts and 5 rnds= 1" in foot patt with D hook

FINISHED DIMENSIONS
(with Sock Folded Flat)

Due to stitch patt structure, sock has approx 1" to 1½" stretch.

Circumference of leg (unstretched): 7½ (8¼, 9, 9¾)"

Circumference of foot (unstretched): 7½ (8¼, 9, 9¾)"

Floor to cuff: 7½"

CUFF

Do not sl st rnds closed and do not ch 1 at beg of rnds and rows unless instructed.

Foundation rnd: With D hook, and with color D, ch 3 (counts as first dc), dcf in 3rd ch from hook, work additional 38 (42, 46, 50) dcf, sl st in top ch of beg ch 3 to close rnd. [40 (44, 48, 52) dcf]

Rnd 1: *FPdc around next 2 dc, dc in next 2 dc; rep from * around, sl st in first st.

Rnd 2: *FPdc around next 2 FPdc, dc in next 2 dc; rep from * around. With A, sl st in first st.

LEG

Work 1 rnd of each color in following sequence: A, B, C, D. As you make your first dc in the rnd, go under all strands of unused colors to bring them up to next rnd. Do not cut yarn after each rnd unless instructed.

Rnd 1: With A, ch 3, dc in first st, *sk next st, 2 dc in next st; rep from * around, sl st in top ch of beg ch 3. Changing to B, sl st between first 2 dc. [40 (44, 48, 52) dc]

Rnd 2: Make a long ch 1 (approx ½" long), 2 dc between first 2 dc of previous rnd, *sk next 2 dc, 2 dc between next 2 dc of previous rnd; rep from * around, sl st in first dc of rnd. With next color, sl st between first 2 dc.

Rep rnd 2 with C and D, then cont in A through D color sequence until leg measures 5", ending with D. Except for D, cut all other colors.

HEEL OPENING

Next rnd: Change to E hook and with D loosely ch 20 (22, 24, 26). Change back to D hook, sk next 20 (22, 24, 26) sts, sc in next 20 (22, 24, 26) sts, sc in each ch, sl st in next sc. [40 (44, 48, 52) sc]

FOOT

Rnd 1: With D, *hdc in next 3 sts, ch 1, sk next st; rep from * around. With A, sl st in first hdc.

Rnd 2: With A, *sc in next 3 sts, esc in skipped st on previous rnd; rep from * around. With color D, sl st in first st.

Rep rnds 1 and 2 until sock measures 2" from longest toe, ending with rnd 2.

TOE

Rnd 1: With D, sc in each st around.

Rnd 2: With C, sc in each st, around.

Fold sock to position heel opening correctly on bottom of foot (see page 62). PM on each side edge of sock. Move markers with each rnd to keep at side edges of toe.

Rnd 3: *Sc to 2 sts prior to marker, sc2tog, sc in marked st, sc2tog; rep from * once, sc in rem sts. [36 (40, 44, 48) sc] Rep rnds 2 and 3 until 24 (28, 32, 36) sts rem. Fasten off, sew toe.

AFTERTHOUGHT HEEL

Fold sock to position toe correctly on foot (see page 7).

Rnd 1: Attach C to bottom of foot at middle of heel opening. Sc in each st to corner, 2 sc in first corner, working in bottom leg section, sc in next 20 (22, 24, 26) sts, 2 sc in next corner, sc in rem sts. [44 (48, 52, 56) sc] PM on each side edge of heel opening, ensuring the same number of sts on bottom and top. Move markers with each rnd to keep at side edges.

Rnd 2: *Sc to 2 sts prior to marker, sc2tog, sc in marked st, sc2tog; rep from * once, sc in rem sts. [40 (44, 48, 52) sc]

Rep rnd 2 until 12 sts rem. Fasten off, sew heel.

Cotton-Candy Confection

Designed by Janet Rehfeldt

Soft shades and delectable textures combine to create a confection of beauty. The lace-weight yarn crochets into airy cable stitches that swirl and fluff like cotton candy. The simple texture of the foot continues the soft yet elegant design with just the hint of a lacy latticework, and although raised on the right side, the texture against your skin is smooth and comfortable.

Skill level: Experienced ◀■■■▶

FEATURED TECHNIQUES

* Toe-up method
* Short-row heel

MATERIALS

1 skein of Anne from Schaefer Yarn (60% merino wool superwash, 25% mohair, 15% nylon; 113 g/4 oz; 560 yds/512 m) in color Snooks (0)

Size D-3 (3.25 mm) crochet hook or size required for gauge

3 stitch markers

GAUGE

6.5 sts and 5.5 rnds = 1" in foot patt

FINISHED DIMENSIONS

(with Sock Folded Flat)

Circumference of leg (unstretched): 6¾ (7¾, 8¾, 9¾)"

Circumference of foot (unstretched): 6½ (7⅛, 8, 9¼)"

Floor to cuff: 8"

NOTE:

Do not sl st rnds closed and do not ch 1 at beg of rnds and rows unless instructed.

SPECIAL STITCH

Modified half double crochet (mhdc): YO, insert hook into next st, YO, pull through st and first lp on hook, YO, pull through 2 lps on hook.

Cable 6 stitches to the back (C6B): Sk next 3 sts, dtr in next 3 sts, working behind but not catching dtrs just worked, dtr in skipped sts.

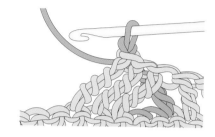

Cable 6 stitches to the front (C6F): Sk next 3 sts, dtr in next 3 sts, working in front but not catching dtrs just worked, dtr in skipped sts.

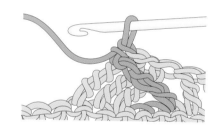

TOE

Foundation row: Ch 9 (10, 11, 11), working in bottom lp, sl st in second ch from hook, sl st in each ch. [8 (9, 10, 10) sl sts]

Rnd 1: Working in top lps of beg ch, sc in each ch, pivot work, sc in each sl st of foundation row. PM at each end to mark side edges of toe. Move markers with each rnd to keep at side edges of toe. [16 (18, 20, 20) sc]

Rnd 2: *Mhdc to 1 st prior to side marker, 2 hdc in next st, mhdc in marked st, 2 hdc in next st; rep from * once. [20 (22, 24, 24) sts]

Rep rnd 2 until you have 40 (46, 52, 60) sts.

FOOT

Next rnd: Mhdc in each st around.

Rep last rnd until foot reaches just below anklebone or approx 2½" shorter than desired foot length.

HEEL

Row 1: Fold sock to position toe correctly on foot (see page 7). Work in patt to a side edge, mhdc in next 0 (0, 1, 2) sts, PM in last mhdc to mark top of foot, sl st in next st, sc in same st as sl st, sc in next 19 (21, 23, 25) sts, PM in next mhdc to mark top of foot, turn. [20 (22, 24, 26) sc] Rem sts unworked.

Row 2 (WS): Ch 1, sc in first sc, sc in each sc across, leaving last st unworked, turn. [19 (21, 23, 25) sc]

Rep row 2 until 8 (10, 12, 14) sc rem.

HEEL INCREASE

Row 1 (WS): Sc in 8 (10, 12, 14) sc, sc in side edge of heel, sc in closest sk st on heel, sl st in side edge of heel, turn. [10 (12, 14, 16) sc]

Row 2: Sk sl st, sc in 10 (12, 14, 16,) sc, sc in closest sk st on heel, sc in next closest sk st on heel, sl st in side edge of heel, turn. [12 (14, 16, 18) sc]

Row 3: Sk sl st, sc in 12 (14, 16, 18,) sc, sc in closest sk st on heel, sl st in side edge of heel, turn. [13 (15, 17, 19) sc]

Rows 4–8: Rep row 3. [18 (20, 22, 24) sc at end of row 8]

Row 9: Sk sl st, sc in 18 (20, 22, 24) sc, sc in closest sk st on heel, sc in side edge at base at heel, sl st in marked st at top of foot, turn. [20 (22, 24, 26) sc]

Row 10: Sk sl st, sc in 20 (22, 24, 26) sc, sc in closest sk st on heel, sc in side edge at base of heel, sl st in marked st at top of foot; do not turn. [22 (24, 26, 28) sc]

LEG

Rnd 1: Mhdc in marked st on top of foot, mhdc in rem 19 (23, 27, 33) top foot sts, sk sl st at heel, mhdc in 22 (24, 26, 28) sc of heel, sk last sl st, PM for beg of rnd. [42 (48, 54, 62) mhdc]

Rnd 2: Mhdc in each st around.

Rnd 3: Mhdc around and evenly inc 3 (7, 6, 4) sts. [45 (55, 60, 66) mhdc]

Rnd 4: *Dc in next 1 (2, 2, 2) sts, FPtr around next 1 (1, 2, 1) st, dc in next 1 (2, 2, 2) sts, C6B; rep from * around, sl st in first dc.

Rnd 5: *Dc in next 1 (2, 2, 2) sts, FPtr around next 1 (1, 2, 1) sts, dc in next 1 (2, 2, 2) sts, C6F; rep from * around, sl st in first dc.

Rep rnds 4 and 5 five more times. Fasten off.

Double-treble secret:

The secret to double-treble-crochet cables is an even and slightly snug tension, and taking it slow and easy when working the loops off the hook.

A Moment of Zen

Designed by Janet Rehfeldt

Open heeled and toeless, these socks are great for your stretch and yoga exercises. The soft yarn is treated with jojoba oil and/or aloe vera, making the socks soft and comforting for that moment of Zen we all need in our hectic lives. Add an afterthought heel and a strip for between the toes, and you have the perfect sock for sandals or a trip to the spa.

Skill level: Easy ◖■◻◻

FEATURED TECHNIQUES

* Top-down method
* Sideways slip-stitch cuff
* Optional afterthought heel

MATERIALS

Yoga Sock

1 skein of Step from Austermann (75% superwash virgin wool, 25% nylon; 100 g/3.5 oz; 459 yds/420 m) in color 010 (1)

Size E-4 (3.5 mm) crochet hook or size required for gauge

1 stitch marker

Spa Sock

2 (2, 3, 3, 3) skeins of Heart & Sole from Coats & Clark (70% superwash wool, 30% nylon; 50 g/1.75 oz; 213 yds/195 m) in color 3972 Blackjack (1)

Size D-3 (3.25 mm) crochet hook for optional afterthought heel and toe strap

Size E-4 (3.5 mm) crochet hook for cuff, leg, and foot or size required for gauge

3 stitch markers

GAUGE

5.25 sts and 5 rnds = 1" in esc with E hook

FINISHED DIMENSIONS

(with Sock Folded Flat)

Circumference of leg (unstretched): 6¼ (7⅜, 8½, 9⅝, 10⅝)"

Circumference of foot (unstretched): 6¼ (7⅜, 8½, 9⅝, 10⅝)"

Floor to cuff: 8"

Do not sl st rnds closed, and do not ch 1 at beg of rnds and rows unless instructed. For matching socks, beg with the same color sequence.

CUFF

Row 1: With E hook, ch 11, bl sl st in 2nd ch from hook, bl sl st in each ch across, turn. [10 sl sts]

Row 2: Ch 1, bl sl st in first sl st, bl sl st in each sl st across, turn.

Rep row 2 until cuff measures approx 6 (7, 8, 9¼, 10¼)".

LEG

Pivot cuff to work on long side edge of cuff.

Rnd 1: Work 32 (38, 44, 50, 56) sc evenly spaced along cuff. Bring short ends of cuff tog, matching ends to form a circle, join with sl st in first sc. Sew cuff closed (see page 62).

Rnd 2: Esc in each st around.

Rep rnd 2 until piece measures 6" from beg. Sl st in first esc on last rnd to close rnd.

ANKLE

Rnds 1–3: *FPdc around next st, hdc in next st; rep from * around.

HEEL OPENING

Rnd 1: Work in (FPdc, hdc) patt across 16 (19, 22, 25, 28) sts, ch 16 (19, 22, 25, 28), sk next 16 (19, 22, 25, 28) sts. [16 (19, 22, 25, 28) sts; 16 (19, 22, 25, 28) chs]

Rnd 2: Work in (FPdc, hdc) patt across 16 (19, 22, 25, 28) top foot sts, hdc in bottom lp of next 16 (19, 22, 25, 28) chs. [32 (38, 44, 50, 56) sts]

Rnds 3 and 4: Work in (FPdc, hdc) patt, sl st in first st on last rnd to close rnd.

FOOT

Rnd 1: Esc in each st around. [32 (38, 44, 50, 56) esc]

Rep rnd 1 until foot measures 2¾" to 3" from longest toe.

Next rnd: Fold sock so that heel opening is positioned correctly on back of sock. PM at each side edge. Esc to first marker, sc2tog, esc to next marker, sc2tog, esc in rem sts. [30 (36, 42, 48, 54) sts]

Next rnd: Sc in each st around. Fasten off.

OPTIONAL AFTERTHOUGHT HEEL

Fold sock so heel opening is positioned correctly on back of sock foot. PM at each side edge, move markers with each rnd to keep at side edge of heel.

Rnd 1: Change to D hook, attach yarn at center point of opening on leg section, evenly sc 40 (46, 52, 58, 64) around opening.

Rnds 2 and 3: Sc in each st around.

Rnd 4: *Sc to 2 sts prior to first marker, sc2tog, sc in marked st, sc2tog; rep from * once, sc in rem sts. [36 (42, 48, 54, 60) sc]

Rep rnd 4 until 12 (14, 16, 18, 20) sts rem. Fasten off, sew heel.

TOE STRIP

Row 1: With D hook, ch 4, sc in 2nd ch from hook and in each ch, turn. [3 sc]

Row 2: Ch 1, sc in each sc, turn.

Rep row 2 until strip is long enough to fit snugly, but comfortably, between large and second toes. Fasten off. Position strip on sock, sew in place.

A Walk on the Bright Side

Designed by Mary Jane Wood

Blocks of contrasting stripes highlight the feet and legs of these socks and will have you taking a walk on the bright side. The pattern is an easy combination of single crochet and chain one. Color changes are minimized since only one color is used at a time and yarns are carried up rather than cut after each round. The yarn used in this project may feel slightly harsh at first; however, once washed and blocked, the yarn is extremely soft and durable.

Skill level: Intermediate ◼◼◼▢

FEATURED TECHNIQUES

* Toe-up method
* Afterthought heel

MATERIALS

Pair of Sox from Sandy's Palette (80% wool 20% nylon; 113 g/4 oz; 430 yds/393 m) in the following colors 1

MC 1 skein in color Violet

CC 1 skein in color Lime

Size D-3 (3.25 mm) crochet hook for leg, heel, and foot or size required for gauge

Size E-4 (3.5 mm) crochet hook for making chain over heel opening

3 stitch markers

GAUGE

4.33 sts and 5.5 rnds =1" in leg and foot patt with D hook

FINISHED DIMENSIONS

(with Sock Folded Flat)

Stitch structure allows 1½" to 2" stretch

Circumference of leg (unstretched): 7⅓ (8⅓, 9¼, 10¼)"

Circumference of foot (unstretched): 7⅓ (8⅓, 9¼, 10¼)"

Floor to cuff: 8"

NOTE:

Do not sl st rnds closed and do not ch 1 at beg of rnds and rows unless instructed.

TOE

Foundation row: With D hook and MC, ch 9 (11, 13, 15), working in bottom lp, sl st in second ch from hook, sl st in each ch. [8 (10, 12, 14) sl sts]

Rnd 1: Working in top lps of beg ch, sc in each ch, pivot work, sc in each sl st of foundation row. PM at each end to mark side edges of toe. Move markers with each rnd to keep at side edges. [16 (20, 24, 28) sc]

Rnd 2: *Sc to 1 st prior to marker, 2 sc in next st, sc in marked st, 2 sc in next st; rep from * once.[20 (24, 28, 32)]

Rnd 3: Sc in each st.

Rnds 4–9: Rep rnds 2 and 3. [32 (36, 40, 44) sc at end of rnd 9] Remove markers.

Rnds 10 and 11: Sc in each st.

FOOT

To eliminate joining lines in foot and leg when working rnds 1–24, after completing 8 rnds, sl st in next 5 sts. Start next rnd in the 6th st, marking this as first st in rnd.

Rnd 1: With MC, sc in first st, *ch 1, sc in next st; rep from * around, changing to CC in last sc. PM to mark beg of rnds. [32 (36, 40, 44) sc; 32 (36, 40, 44) ch-1 sps]

Rnd 2: With CC, sc in each ch-1 sp, skipping all sc, sl st in first sc, changing to MC. [32 (36, 40, 44) sc]

Rnds 3–8: Rep rnds 1 and 2. At end of rnd 8 do not change to MC, sl st in next 5 sts.

Rnd 9: With CC, sc in next sc, PM for new beg of rnds, *ch 1, sc in next st; rep from * around, changing to MC in last st.

Rnd 10: With MC, sc in each ch-1 sp, skipping all sc, sl st in first sc, changing to CC.

Rnds 11–16: Rep rnds 9 and 10. At end of rnd 16 do not change to CC, sl st in next 5 sts.

Rnds 17–24: If sock measures 1" short of anklebone, jump to rnd 25; otherwise, rep rows 1–8 once; then go to rnd 25.

Rnd 25: With CC, *sc in next st, dc in next st; rep from * around.

Rnd 26: *Dc in next sc, sc in next dc; rep from * around.

Rep rnds 25 and 26 until foot reaches just below anklebone or 2" shorter than desired foot length.

HEEL OPENING

Fold sock to position toe correctly on foot (see page 7). Work in established patt to side edge of foot.

Change to E hook and CC, ch 16 (18, 20, 22) loosely. Change back to D hook, sk next 16 (18, 20, 22) sts, sc in next 16 (18, 20, 22) sts, sc in 16 (18, 20, 22) ch. With MC, sl st in next sc. [32 (36, 40, 44) sc]

LEG

Mark first st of each rnd.

Rnd 1: With MC, sc in same st as last sl st and in each st around leg and heel. [32 (36, 40, 44) sc]

Rnds 2–17: Cont in established foot patt, rep rnds 1–16 until sock leg measures approx 6".

CUFF

Rnd 1: With MC, dc in each st around. [32 (36, 40, 44) dc]

Rnd 2: *FPdc around next dc, dc in next dc; rep from * around. [32 (36, 40, 44) sts]

Rnd 3: *FPdc around next FPdc, dc in next dc; rep from * around, sl st in first st.

Fasten off and weave in all ends.

AFTERTHOUGHT HEEL

Fold sock to position toe correctly on foot (see page 7).

Rnd 1 (RS): Attach MC to bottom of foot at center point of heel opening. Sc in each st to corner, 2 sc in corner, working in bottom of ch, sc in next 16 (18, 20, 22) sts, 2 sc in next corner, sc in rem sts. PM in each corner, having the same number of sts on bottom and top. Move markers with each rnd to keep at side edges. [36 (40, 44, 48) sc]

Rnd 2: *Sc in each st to 2 sts prior to marker, sc2tog, sc in marked st, sc2tog; rep from * once, sc in rem sts. [32 (36, 40, 44) sc]

Rep rnd 2 until 12 sts rem. Fasten off, sew heel.

Way Beyond the Blue

Designed by Janet Rehfeldt

Extremely delicate waves and color tones in this lace-weight yarn bring to mind images of a tropical paradise. Waves along the leg flowing seamlessly into the foot; an ocean's reef floating along way beyond the blue . . . and it's oh so simple. The ripple pattern lends itself extremely well to most shaded tonal colors as well as solids.

Skill level: Easy ◼◼☐☐

FEATURED TECHNIQUES

* Top-down method
* Heel flap with gusset

MATERIALS

1 skein of Anne from Schaefer Yarn (60% merino wool, 25% mohair, 15% nylon; 113 g/4 oz; 560 yds/512 m) in color Bugs (0)

C-2 (2.75 mm) crochet hook for heel and toe

D-3 (3.25 mm) crochet hook for leg and foot or size required for gauge

3 stitch markers

GAUGE

7 sts and 4 rnds = 1" in leg patt with D hook

FINISHED DIMENSIONS

(with Sock Folded Flat)

Circumference of leg (unstretched): 6⅜ (7½, 8⅝, 9⅞)"

Circumference of foot (unstretched): 6⅜ (7½, 8⅝, 9⅞)"

Floor to cuff: 8"

SPECIAL STITCH

Puff stitch: YO, insert hook into st, YO, pull through st, YO, pull through 2 lps, YO, insert hook into same st, YO, pull through st, YO, pull through 2 lps, YO, pull through 3 lps.

> **NOTE:**
>
> Do not ch 1 at beg of rnds and do not sl st rnds closed unless instructed. Work (dc, puff st, dc) through both lps of puff st in previous rnd.

LEG

Rnd 1: With D hook, ch 3 (counts as first dc), dcf in 3rd ch from hook, work additional 42 (50, 58, 66) dcf, sl st in 3rd ch of beg ch 3 to close rnd. PM for beg of rnds. [44 (52, 60, 68) sts]

Rnd 2: *Esc in next 4 (5, 6, 7) sts, sk 2 sts, esc in next 4 (5, 6, 7) sts, (dc, puff st, dc) in next st; rep from * around. [44 (52, 60, 68) sts]

Rnd 3: *Bl esc in next 4 (5, 6, 7) sts, sk 2 sts, bl esc in next 4 (5, 6, 7) sts, (dc, puff st, dc) in both lps of next st; rep from * around. [44 (52, 60, 68) sts]

Rep rnds 2 and 3 until piece measures 5" from beg.

HEEL FLAP

Row 1: PM in last dc worked in previous rnd, change to C hook, sl st in next esc, sc in same st, sc in next 21 (25, 29, 33) sts, PM in next esc, turn. [22 (26, 30, 34) sc] Rem sts unworked

Row 2 (WS): Ch 1, sc in each st across, turn.

Row 3: Ch 1, sc in first 2 sts, *FPdc around next 2 sts, sc in next 2 sts; rep from * across, turn.

Rep rows 2 and 3 until heel flap measures 2½" to 2¾" from beg, ending with a RS.

HEEL TURN

Row 1 (WS): Ch 1, sc in first sc, sc2tog twice, sc in next 4 (6, 8, 10) sts, sc2tog twice, sc in next 4 (6, 8, 10) sts, sc2tog twice, sc in last sc, turn. [16 (20, 24, 28) sc]

Row 2: Ch 1, sc in first sc, sc2tog twice, sc to last 5 sts, sc2tog twice, sc in last sc, turn. [12 (16, 20, 24) sc]

Row 3: Ch 1, sc in first sc, sc2tog 0 (1, 2, 3) times, sc in next 3 sc, sc2tog 2 times, sc in next 3 sc, sc2tog 0 (1, 2, 3) times, sc in last sc, turn. [10 (12, 14, 16) sc]

Row 4: Ch 1, sc2tog twice, sc to last 5 sts, sc2tog twice, sc in last sc; do not turn. [6 (8, 10, 12) sc]

GUSSET

Rnd 1 (RS): With C hook, evenly work 16 (16, 18, 19) sc along left-side edge of heel flap, PM in last sc made, change to D hook, esc in marked st on front of foot, remove marker, esc in 21 (25, 29, 33) more front foot sts, remove marker in last front foot st, with C hook evenly work 16 (16, 18, 19) sc along right-side edge of heel flap, PM in first sc made, sc in 6 (8, 10, 12) heel sts, PM for beg of rnds. [60 (66, 76, 84) sc]

Rnd 2: With D hook, hdc to 1 st prior to first gusset marker, hdc2tog, hdc to next gusset marker, hdc2tog, hdc in rem sts. [58 (64, 74, 82) hdc]

Rep rnd 2 until 44 (52, 60, 68) sts rem. Remove gusset markers.

FOOT

Work in hdc every rnd until foot measures 2½" from longest toe.

TOE

Fold sock so that heel is positioned correctly on foot (see page 62). PM at each side edge of foot. Move markers with each rnd to keep at side edges.

Next rnd: With C hook, *hdc to 2 sts prior to side marker, sc2tog, hdc in marked st, sc2tog; rep from * once, hdc in rem foot sts. [40 (48, 56, 64) sts]

Rep last rnd until 20 (24, 24, 28) sts rem. Fasten off, sew toe.

CUFF

With D hook, attach yarn to inner side edge at top of leg, loosely sl st in bl of each st around, fasten off.

Buttoned Down

Designed By Janet Rehfeldt

Take fun colors, an easily achieved texture on the foot and leg, add a fold-down cuff in a bright coordinated color, and you've got yourself something uniquely different and loads of fun. Button accents finish off this sock that can't help shouting, "Hey, look at me!"

Skill level: Easy ■■□□

FEATURED TECHNIQUES

* Toe-up method
* Afterthought heel
* Fold-down cuff

MATERIALS

A 2 skeins of Flusi Color from Regia (75% superwash wool, 25% polyamide; 50 g/1.75oz; 229 yds/210m) in color 01800 multi [1]

B 1 skein of Regia Classic 4 Fold from Regia (75% superwash wool, 25% polyamide; 50 g/1.75 oz; 229 yds/210m) in color 01092 green [1]

Size D-3 (3.25 mm) crochet hook for toe, rib, heel, and cuff

Size E-4 (3.5 mm) crochet hook for foot and leg or size required for gauge

3 stitch markers

16 multicolored buttons, ¼" diameter

GAUGE

6.5 hdc and 4 rnds = 1" in patt with E hook

FINISHED DIMENSIONS

(with Sock Folded Flat)

Circumference of leg (unstretched): 6¼ (7½, 8½, 9⅝)"

Circumference of foot (unstretched): 6¼ (7½, 8¾, 9⅝)"

Floor to cuff: 7" with cuff up

NOTE:

Do not sl st rnds closed and do not ch 1 at beg of rnds or rows unless instructed.

TOE

Foundation row: With D hook and A, ch 8 (9, 10, 12), working in bottom lp, sl st in second ch from hook, sl st in each ch. [7 (8, 9, 11) sl sts]

Rnd 1: Working in top lps of beg ch, sc in each ch, pivot work, sc in each sl st of foundation row. PM at each end to mark side edges of toe. Move markers with each rnd to keep at sides edges. [14 (16, 18, 22) sc]

Rnds 2–4: *Sc to 1 st prior to side marker, 2 sc in next sc, 1 sc in marked st, 2 sc in next st; rep from * once. [26 (28, 30, 34) sc at end of rnd 4]

Rnd 5: Sc in each st around.

Rnd 6: *Sc to 1 st prior to side marker, 2 sc in next sc, sc in marked st, 2 sc in next st; rep from * once. [30 (32, 34, 38) sc]

Rep rnds 5 and 6 until 42 (48, 54, 62) sts rem, on last rnd sl st in first sc of rnd. Remove side-edge markers.

FOOT

Next rnd: With E hook, *fl hdc in next 2 sts, bl hdc in next 2 sts; rep from * around.

Rep last rnd until foot reaches just below anklebone or approx 2½" shorter than desired foot length.

HEEL OPENING

Rnd 1: Fold sock, positioning toe correctly on sock (see page 7), work in patt to side edge. Work in patt over next 20 (24, 26, 30) sts, loosely ch 22 (24, 28, 32), sk next 22 (24, 28, 32) sts. [20 (24, 26, 30) hdc; 22 (24, 28, 32) chs]

Rnd 2: Work in patt over 20 (24, 26, 30) front foot sts; working in bottom lp of ch, hdc in 22 (24, 28, 32) chs around heel opening. [42 (48, 54, 62) hdc]

Rnd 3: Work in patt over 20 (24, 26, 30) front foot sts, cont in established front-and-back-lp hdc patt in 22 (24, 28, 32) hdc over heel.

LEG

With E hook, work in established front-and-back-lp hdc patt until leg measures 5" from heel opening.

Next rnd: Hdc in each st around.

Next rnd: Change to D hook, *FPdc around next st, hdc in next st; rep from * around.

Rep last rnd twice, on final rnd sl st in first dc of rnd. Fasten off.

AFTERTHOUGHT HEEL

Rnd 1: Fold sock so toe is positioned correctly (see page 7). Change to D hook, attach B at center back of heel opening, making sure to work under both lps of the sts, evenly work 44 (50, 56, 64) sc around heel opening, PM at side edges of heel. Move side markers with each rnd to keep at side edges.

Rnd 2: *Sc to 2 sts prior to side-edge marker, sc2tog, sc in marked st, sc2tog; *rep from * once. [40 (46, 52, 60) sc]

Rep rnd 2 until 12 (14, 16, 16) sts rem, work to side edge of heel. Fasten off, sew heel.

CUFF

Row 1: Fold sock so heel is positioned correctly (see page 62). With D hook, attach B to top of leg at right-side edge for right sock, left-side edge for left sock with sl st, sc in same st as join, sc in next 2 sts, sc2tog, sc in rem sts, turn. [41 (47, 53, 61) sc]

Row 2: Ch 1, (sc, ch 1, dc) in first st, sk next st, *(sc, ch 1, dc) in next st, sk next st; rep from * to last st, sc in last st, turn.

Row 3: Ch 1, (sc, ch 1, dc) in first sc, sk next dc and ch-1 sp, *(sc, ch 1, dc) in next sc, sk next dc and ch-1 sp; rep from * to last sc, sk last sc, sc in beg ch 1 of previous row, turn.

Rep row 3 until cuff is 2". Fasten off.

Fold cuff down and sew 4 buttons on each side edge of cuff.

No-Shows and Paint My Toes

These little half socks are perfect for slip-ons, mules, clogs, and Birkenstocks. Made with cotton/elastic yarn, they're comfy and just the ticket for when you want to have something between you and your slip-ons, but don't want a full sock. The variation of toe sections convert these little numbers to a pedi-sock, great for sandals, flip-flops, or for pampering your feet and toes at the spa.

Skill level: Easy ◖◼◻◻

FEATURED TECHNIQUES

* Top-down method
* Double-crochet-foundation-stitch cuff

MATERIALS

No-Shows

1 skein of Fixation from Cascade Yarns (98.3% cotton, 1.7% elastic; 50 g/1.75 oz; 100 yds/130 m) in color 5363 teal

Paint My Toes

1 skein of Fixation from Cascade Yarns in color 9490 multi

Both Styles

Size D-3 (3.25 mm) crochet hook for cuff

Size E-4 (3.5 mm) crochet hook or size required for gauge

3 stitch markers

GAUGE

5.75 sts and 4.5 rnds = 1" in patt with E hook

FINISHED DIMENSIONS

Your sock should fit snug but comfortably. Elastic yarn has 1½" to 2" stretch allowance.

Circumference of foot (unstretched): 6 (7, 8, 9)"

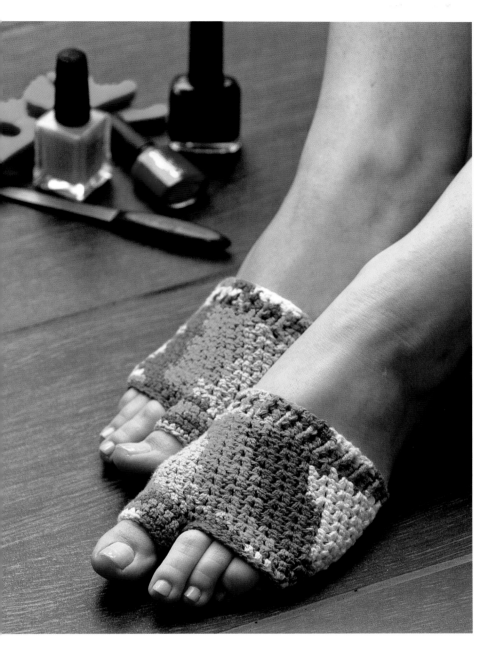

Foot

Rnd 1: Change to E hook, work 2 esc in first st, sk next st, *2 esc in next st, sk next st; rep from * around. [34 (40, 46, 52) esc]

Rnd 2: Work 2 esc between first 2 esc (V st made), *V st between next 2 esc; rep from * around.

Rnd 3: *V st in V st from previous rnd; rep from * around.

Rep rnd 3 until piece measures 3½" from beg.

Toe

Remove beg-of-rnd marker. Fold sock flat. PM at each side edge of foot. Move side markers with each rnd to keep at side edges. Work to center back of foot, PM for new beg of rnds.

Next rnd: *Esc to 2 sts prior to side-edge marker, sc2tog, sc in marked st, sc2tog; rep from * once, esc in rem sts. [30 (36, 42, 48) hdc]

Rep last rnd until 10 (12, 14, 16) sts rem, work to closest side-edge marker, sl st in marked st. Fasten off, sew toe.

PAINT MY TOES

Work as for No-Shows until foot measures 3" from beg. Remove beg-of-rnd marker. Fold sock flat, keeping beg seam of cuff at a side edge or bottom of foot. PM at each side edge of foot. Cont with following instructions.

Left-Foot Large Toe

Rnd 1: Esc to left-side edge, esc in marked st, esc in 6 (7, 8, 9) sts, ch 3 for bridge between toes, sl st in 6 (7, 8, 9)th st counted

NO-SHOWS

Cuff

Rnd 1: With D hook, ch 3 (counts as first dc), dcf in 3rd ch from hook, work additioinal 32 (38, 44, 50) dcf, sl st in 3rd ch of beg ch 3 to form a circle and close rnd. [34 (40, 46, 52) dcf]

Rnds 2 and 3: FPdc around first st, PM for beg of rnds, hdc in next st, *FPdc around next st, hdc in next st; rep from* around. [34 (40, 46, 52) sts]

backward from left-side marker. [13 (15, 17, 19) esc, 3 chs]

Rnd 2: Esc in 13 (15, 17, 19) esc, esc in 3 chs. [16 (18, 20, 22) esc]

Rnds 3 and 4: Esc in each esc.

Rnd 5: Esc to center back of toe, sc in each st around. Fasten off.

Left-Foot Remaining Toe Area

With toe at left side of sock, attach yarn at center back of rem toes area, PM.

Rnd 1: Esc to toe bridge, sc in bottom of 3 toe-bridge sts, esc to 2 sts prior to right-edge marker,

sc2tog, esc in marked st, sc2tog, esc in rem sts on foot. [22 (26, 30, 34) sts]

Rnd 2: Esc to 2 sts prior to right-edge marker, sc2tog, esc in marked st, sc2tog, esc in rem sts on foot. [20 (24, 28, 32) sts]

Rnd 3: Sl st in each st around. Fasten off.

Right-Foot Large Toe

Rnd 1: PM at each side edge, esc to right-side edge, esc in marked st, esc in 6 (7, 8, 9) sts, ch 3 for bridge between toes, sl st in 6 (7, 8, 9)th st counted

backward from right-side marker. [13 (15, 17, 19) esc, 3 chs]

Work rnds 2–5 as for left-foot large toe.

Right-Foot Remaining Toe Area

With toe at right side of sock, attach yarn at center back of rem toes area, PM.

Rnd 1: Esc to 2 sts prior to left-edge marker, sc2tog, esc in marked st, sc2tog, esc to toe, sc in bottom of 3 toe-bridge sts, esc in rem sts. [22 (26, 30, 34) sts]

Rnds 2 and 3: Rep rnds 2 and 3 of left-foot remaining toe area.

Shown in color 9349 coral.

Shown in color 9980 multi.

Flip My Flops

Designed by Carol Lykins and Janet Rehfeldt

Who says sandals and flip-flops are only for summer? With these comfy split-toe socks, you'll be donning your flip-flops all year round. The stretchiness of the stitch structure and yarn allow this sock to fit a good range of foot widths. The design and stitch technique are suited for variegated, hand-painted, and solid colorways.

Skill level: Intermediate ◖■■■◻

FEATURED TECHNIQUES

* Top-down method
* Sideways slip-stitch cuff
* Heel flap with gusset
* Split toe

MATERIALS

1 skein of Denali from Pagewood Farm (80% merino superwash wool, 20% nylon; 113 g/4 oz; 450 yds/411 m) in color Peaceful (1)

Size D-3 (3.25 mm) crochet hook for heel flap, gusset, and toe

Size E-4 (3.5 mm) crochet hook for cuff, leg, and foot or size required for gauge

GAUGE

5.75 sts and 4 rnds = 1" in patt st with E hook

FINISHED DIMENSIONS

(with Sock Folded Flat)

Stitch structure allows for 1¼" to 1¾" stretch in width.

Circumference of leg (unstretched): 6 (7¼, 8⅜, 9⅜)"

Circumference of foot (unstretched): 6 (7¼, 8⅜, 9⅜)"

Floor to cuff: 8"

SPECIAL STITCHES

Modified half double crochet (mhdc): YO, insert hook through bl of next st, YO, pull through st and 1 lp on hook, YO, pull through last 2 lps on hook.

Modified half double crochet decrease (mhdc2tog): YO, insert hook through bl of next st, YO, pull up a lp (3 lps on hook), insert hook through bl of next st, YO, pull through bl and 2 lps on hook, YO, pull through last 2 lps on hook.

CUFF

Row 1: With E hook, ch 7, bl sl st in 2nd ch from hook, bl sl st in each ch, turn. [6 sl sts]

Row 2: Ch 1, bl sl st in each st across, turn. [6 sl st]

Rep row 2 until piece measures 6 (7, 8, 9)".

LEG

Pivot cuff to work on long edge.

Rnd 1: Work 36 (42, 48, 54) hdc evenly spaced along cuff. Bring short ends tog to form a circle, join with sl st in first hdc. Sew cuff closed (see page 62).

> **NOTE:**
>
> Patt st is worked in bl only unless otherwise instructed. Do not sl st rnds closed and do not beg rnds or rows with ch 1 unless otherwise instructed.

Rnd 2: Bl mhdc in each st around.

Rep rnd 2 until leg measures 5" including cuff.

HEEL

Row 1: Change to D hook, sc in next 17 (19, 21, 23) sts, turn. Rem sts unworked.

Row 2: Ch 1, sc each sc across, turn.

Rep row 2 until heel measures 2½" to 2¾", ending with a RS row.

HEEL TURN

Row 1 (WS): Ch 1, sc in first sc, sc2tog twice, sc in next 2 (3, 4, 5) sc, sc2tog twice, sc in next 1 (2, 3, 4) sc, sc2tog twice, sc in last sc, turn. [11 (13, 15, 17) sc]

Rows 2–4: Ch 1, sc in first sc, sc2tog, sc to last 3 sc, sc2tog, sc in last sc. Do not turn. [5 (7, 9, 11) sc at end of row 4]

GUSSET

Rnd 1: Work 18 sc evenly spaced along left edge of heel flap, PM, work mhdc across 19 (23, 27, 31) front foot sts, work 18 sc evenly spaced along right edge of heel flap, PM in first sc on right side of heel flap, sc in 5 (7, 9, 11) heel sts, PM in last sc made to mark beg of rnds. [60 (66, 72, 78) sc]

Rnd 2: Mhdc in each st around. [60 (66, 72, 78) mhdc]

Rnd 3: Mhdc to 3 sts prior to first gusset marker, mhdc2tog twice, mhdc across foot front to next gusset marker, mdc2tog twice, mhdc in rem heel sts. [56 (62, 68, 74) mhdc]

Rep rnds 2 and 3 until 36 (42, 48, 54) sts rem; end with rnd 3. Remove gusset markers.

FOOT

Next rnd: Change to E hook, mhdc in each st around. [36 (42, 48, 54) sts]

Rep last rnd until foot measures 2" from longest toe.

RIGHT-SOCK BIG TOE

Fold sock flat so heel is positioned correctly (see page 62). PM in each side st. Work in mhdc to 1 st prior to right side-edge marker, sc in right marked st. (Front of sock will be facing you.)

Rnd 1: With D hook, sc in next 5 (6, 7, 8) sts, ch 3, join with sc in the 7 (8, 9, 10)th st from right-side marker on front of foot, sc in next 6 (7, 8, 9) sts. [12 (14, 16, 18) sc and 3 chs]

Rnd 2: Sc to ch 3, sc in each ch, sc in rem sc of toe. [15 (17, 19, 21) sc]

Rnd 3: Sc in each st around.

Rep rnd 3 until toe measures ¼" from end of big toe.

Next rnd: Sc in 1 (0, 1, 1) sc, sc2tog, *sc in next sc, sc2tog; rep from * around, sc in last 0 (0, 1, 0) st. [10 (11, 13, 14) sc]

Next rnd: Sc in 1 (0, 1, 0) sc, *sc2tog, sc in next sc; rep from * around, sc2tog 1 (0, 1, 0) time. [7 (7, 9, 9) sc]

Last rnd: Sc2tog to last sc, sc in last sc. [4 (4, 5, 5) sc]

Fasten off, sew toe.

RIGHT-SOCK REMAINING TOE AREA

Rnd 1: With back of sock facing you, join with sc in sp between sc and ch-3 of toe bridge, PM for beg of rnds, sc in bottom lp of each ch 3, sc in rem sts. [28 (32, 36, 40) sc]

Rnd 2: Sc to 1 st prior to left-edge marker, sc2tog, sc around to beg marker. [27 (31, 35, 39) sc]

Rep rnd 2, moving left-edge marker with each rnd to keep at side edge until 23 (27, 31, 35) sts rem.

Flatten toe section, move beg marker to right-side edge of rem toe area. Move markers with each rnd to keep at side edges.

Next rnd: Sc to 1 st prior to left-edge marker, sc2tog, sc to 1 st prior to beg marker, sc2tog. [21 (25, 29, 33) sc]

Rep last rnd until 15 (17, 17, 19) sts rem.

Final rnd: Sc to 2 sts prior to left-edge marker, sc2tog twice, sc to 2 sts prior to beg marker, sc2tog once. Join with sl st in sc with beg marker. [12 (14, 14, 16) sc]

Fasten off, sew toe.

LEFT-SOCK BIG TOE AND REMAINING TOE AREA

Fold sock flat so heel is positioned correctly (see page 62). PM in each side st, mhdc to 1 st prior to left side-edge marker, sc in marked st. (Back of sock will be facing you.)

Cont as for right-sock big toe and remaining toe area, substituting back for front and left for right to reverse the direction of toe shaping.

Fasten off, sew toe.

Abbreviations

approx approximately

beg begin(ning)

bl back loop

BPdc back-post double crochet (see page 62)

C6B cable 6 stitches to the back (see page 40)

C6F cable 6 stitches to the front (see page 40)

CC contrasting color

ch(s) chain(s) or chain stitch(es)

ch sp(s) chain space(s)

cont continue(ing)(s)

dc double crochet

dcf double-crochet foundation (see page 61)

dec(s) decrease(s)(ing)

dtr double treble crochet

esc extended single crochet (see page 62)

fl front loop

FPdc front-post double crochet (see page 61)

FPtr front-post treble crochet

hdc half double crochet

hdc2tog half double crochet 2 stitches together (see page 62)—1 stitch decreased

inc increase(ing)(s)

lp(s) loop(s)

MC main color

mhdc modified half double crochet

mhdc2tog modified half double crochet 2 stitches together—1 stitch decreased

mm millimeter(s)

oz ounce(s)

pat pattern(s)

PM place marker

rem remain(ing)(s)

rep(s) repeat(s)

rnd(s) round(s)

RS right side

sc single crochet

sc2tog single crochet 2 stitches together (see page 62)—1 stitch decreased

sk skip

sl st(s) slip stitch(es)

slst2tog slip stitch 2 together (see page 62)—1 stitch decreased

sp(s space(s)

st(s) stitch(es)

to together

tr treble crochet

WS wrong side

YO(s) yarn over(s)

Resources

Contact the following companies to find shops that carry the yarns featured in this book.

Blue Sky Alpacas, Inc.
www.blueskyalpacas.com
Blue Sky Sport Weight Alpaca

Brown Sheep Company, Inc.
www.brownsheep.com
Wildfoote

Cascade Yarns
www.cascadeyarn.com
Fixation

Coats & Clark
www.coatsandclark.com
Heart & Sole

Happy Hands Yarns
www.happyhandsyarn.com
Toe Jamz Sock Yarn

Lion Brand Yarns
www.lionbrand.com
Sock-Ease

Oasis Yarn; DJ International, Inc.
www.oasisyarn.com
Aussie Sock

Pagewood Farm
www.pagewoodfarm.com
Denali

Patons Yarns
www.patonsyarns.com
Stretch Socks

Plymouth Yarns
www.plymouthyarn.com
Sockin' Sox; Happy Feet (Dye For Me) Natural

Sandy's Palette
www.sandyspalette.com
Pair of Sox

Schaefer Yarns
www.schaeferyarn.com
Anne

Skacel Collection, Inc.
www.skacelknitting.com
Distributor for Austerman Step

Westminster Fibers
www.westminsterfibers.com
Distributor for Regia and Regia Classics; Flusi Color

Special Instructions and Stitches

Refer to the following for working in loops, working with markers, and using crochet stitches to create more elastic-like cuff edges, unique textures, and interesting patterns.

WORKING IN LOOPS OF STITCHES

Normally you'll be instructed to work into both loops of a stitch; however, some instructions may have you working into either just the front or back loop of a stitch to create a different look or texture.

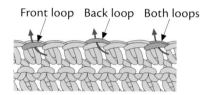

Front loop Back loop Both loops

WORKING WITH MARKERS

The pattern instructions will tell you to place a marker (PM) in a specific stitch or area of the sock to mark the beginning of a round or areas to increase or decrease. For increasing and decreasing, the pattern will instruct you to work up to a specific number of stitches prior to or at the marker. Here's an example: "sc to 3 sts prior to marker." Locate the marker and count back 3 stitches, excluding the stitch with the

marker. Then work the stitches as stated in the directions.

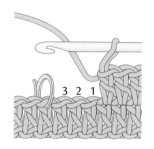

DOUBLE-CROCHET FOUNDATION (DCF)

By starting the cuff of a sock with the double-crochet foundation, you end up with an edge that is more elastic than an edge started with a traditional chain. Ch 3. YO, insert hook into third ch from hook. YO, pull yarn through st.

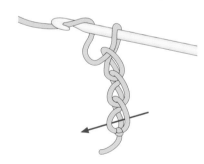

YO, pull yarn through 1 lp on hook (ch 1 made).

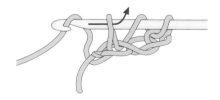

YO, pull yarn through 2 lps on hook.

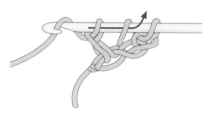

YO, pull yarn through last 2 lps on hook (first dc made). *YO, insert hook through fl and bottom hump of the ch 1.

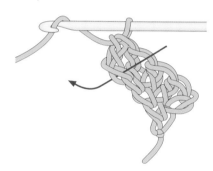

YO, pull yarn through, ch 1, YO, pull yarn through 2 lps on hook, YO, pull yarn through last 2 lps on hook*; rep from * to *, making each new dc in the previous ch.

FRONT-POST DOUBLE CROCHET (FPDC)

YO, insert hook from front to back around indicated dc post, YO, pull yarn through, (YO, pull yarn through 2 lps) 2 times. Always sk st in back of FPdc unless otherwise directed.

BACK-POST DOUBLE CROCHET (BPDC)

YO, insert hook from back to front around indicated dc post, YO, pull yarn through, (YO, pull yarn through 2 lps) 2 times. Always sk st in back of BPdc unless otherwise directed.

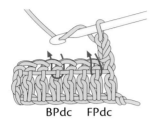

BPdc   FPdc

EXTENDED SINGLE CROCHET (ESC)

Insert hook into next st, YO, pull yarn through st, YO, pull yarn through 1 lp on hook.

YO, pull yarn through 2 lps on hook.

INCREASING AND DECREASING (INC AND DEC)

When increasing, work two stitches into one stitch. When decreasing, work over two stitches.

Single-Crochet Decrease (sc2tog)

Insert hook into next st, YO, pull yarn through st, insert hook into next st, YO, pull yarn through st, YO, pull yarn through all lps on hook.

Half Double Crochet Decrease (hdc2tog)

YO, insert hook into next st, YO, pull yarn through st, insert hook into next st, YO, pull yarn through st, YO, pull yarn through all lps on hook.

Slip-Stitch Decrease (slst2tog)

Insert hook into next st, YO, pull yarn through st, insert hook into next st, YO, pull yarn through all lps on hook.

FINISHING

Once you complete your socks, the last thing you want is a sloppy closure at the toe, afterthought heel, or along the side of the cuff or leg. You want to have a nice, neat finish. One of the best methods for achieving this is to use a mattress seam or invisible seam when sewing the toe or heel closed, or seaming up a sideways cuff and leg.

Sewing the Toe or Afterthought Heel

Fold the sock flat with the heel centered at the back of the foot.

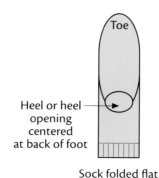

Heel or heel opening centered at back of foot

Sock folded flat

With the right sides of the sock facing out, align the stitches on the front and the back of the toe (or heel). With a large blunt needle and matching yarn, insert the needle under the post and up between 2 stitches, pull the needle through. Go under the post and up between 2 stitches on the opposite side, pull the needle through. Work from one side of the toe (or heel) to the other side of the toe (or heel). Pull yarn up every 3 or 4 stitches to close the stitched portion. Continue in this manner along the edge to be sewn.

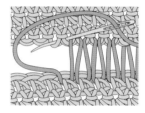

Sewing the Cuff or Leg

Align the side edges of the cuff (or leg) with the right sides facing out. With a large blunt needle and matching yarn, insert the needle under the front loop on one side edge of the cuff (or leg), and then under the back loop on the opposite side edge of the cuff (or leg). Pull the needle and yarn through. Continue in this manner along the edge to be sewn, pulling up yarn every three or four stitches to close the stitched portion.

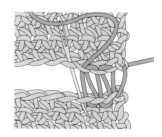

Contributing Designers

Janet would like to acknowledge two very talented and special people
for their contributions to this book.

Mary Jane Wood: I was very happy that Mary Jane, as she did with *Crocheted Socks!*, agreed to contribute several designs to this book. It just would not have been the same had she not agreed to participate. Thank you, Mary Jane, for deciding to work with me again.

Mary Jane learned to crochet from a *McCalls Learn to Crochet* magazine and has been crocheting non-stop for more than 30 years. Her designs have been featured in Dynamic Resource Group publications. She is active in three different California Crochet Guild of America chapters, and she developed and maintains a website for South Bay Crochet, one of her local crochet chapters. Mary Jane is coauthor of *Crocheted Socks!* from Martingale & Company. She lives in San Francisco, California.

Carol Lykins: What a wonderful sister you are. I can always count on you for your help and support. I'm so glad you decided to contribute to this project by both creating a fabulous design and crocheting models before you had to fly off to the far reaches of the earth.

Carol Lykins has been crocheting since she was taught at an early age by our grandmother. She works with me and Knitted Threads Designs as a contract crocheter and pattern editor. We've code-signed many projects over the years, and although Carol likes to stay in the background, she is quite a designer in her own right. Carol and her husband do missionary work around the world. Their home base is in Salem, Oregon.

About the Author

Janet Rehfeldt has been knitting and crocheting since the age of seven. She's the owner of Knitted Threads Designs, LLC, and is an instructor, designer, and author. Her designs and articles can be found in leading knitting and crochet publications, including *Crochet!*, *Crochet Today!*, and *Cast On* magazines; Plymouth Yarn Collection; Skacel Collections, Inc.; Martingale & Company publications; and Dynamic Resource Group publications. She's the author of *Toe-Up Techniques for Hand Knit Socks* (2008) and *Crocheted Socks!* (2003) from Martingale & Company, and she teaches and conducts classes and workshops on both the local and national level. Janet lives in Sun Prairie, Wisconsin, with her husband.

THERE'S MORE ONLINE!

Find more great books on crochet, knitting, and more at www.martingale-pub.com.

You might also enjoy these other fine titles from

Martingale & Company

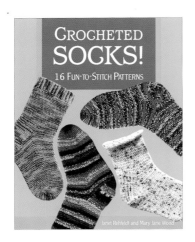

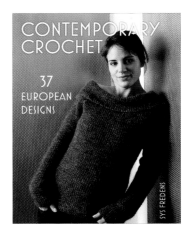

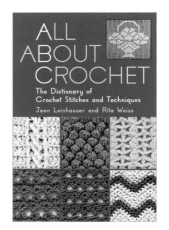

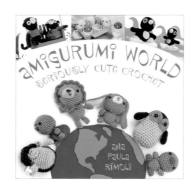

Our books are available at bookstores and your favorite craft, fabric, and yarn retailers.
Visit us at www.martingale-pub.com or contact us at:

1-800-426-3126
International: 1-425-483-3313
Fax: 1-425-486-7596
Email: info@martingale-pub.com

Martingale®
& C O M P A N Y

America's Best-Loved Craft & Hobby Books®
America's Best-Loved Knitting Books®

America's Best-Loved Quilt Books®